ACCEPT NO SUBSTITUTES!

THIS IS THE ONLY GENUINE
1001 VALUABLE THINGS
YOU CAN GET FREE—
AND THE BIGGEST AND THE BEST YET!

For nearly 27 years—since the first edition back in 1955—**1001 Valuable Things You Can Get Free** has sold out fast and furiously, and been cheered by the millions who took advantage of the incredible and fabulous free offers.

Revised again and again, each edition has been printed in larger quantities, and still booksellers have never been able to keep it in stock. It has charmed parents, delighted children and thrilled grandparents, aunts and uncles alike. It's been a boon to teachers on a tight budget. Now here it is in its 12th edition—and it's better than ever!

GALA 12TH EDITION

1001
VALUABLE THINGS
YOU CAN GET FREE

Thelma Weisinger

BANTAM BOOKS
TORONTO · NEW YORK · LONDON · SYDNEY

Notwithstanding continual updating and checking, there may be changes in handling costs, addresses and the like, and we regret any inconvenience which may result.

1001 VALUABLE THINGS YOU CAN GET FREE #12

A Bantam Book / November 1982

ISBN 0-553-22662-2

Published simultaneously in the United States and Canada

Bantam Books are published by Bantam Books, Inc. Its trademark, consisting of the words "Bantam Books" and the portrayal of a rooster, is Registered in U.S. Patent and Trademark Office and in other countries. Marca Registrada. Bantam Books, Inc., 666 Fifth Avenue, New York, New York 10103.

PRINTED IN THE UNITED STATES OF AMERICA

H   0 9 8 7 6 5 4 3 2 1

CONTENTS

HOW TO USE THIS BOOK

1. The free albums, almanacs, atlases, books, brochures, charts, coloring books, decals, dictionaries, films, games, guides, ID cards, kits, magazines, manuals, maps, paintings, patterns, pictures, pinups, plans, portfolios, posters, puzzles, quizzes, recipes, samples, services, stamps, stickers, and all the other items listed in this book are bona fide offers. They represent the choicest giveaways offered by business, industry, nonprofit organizations—and your government.

2. The sponsors of the free items listed in this book, we are assured by the agencies and firms offering them, will be glad to supply them in good faith. *However, each source represented in this book reserves the right to discontinue or withdraw its offer whenever it sees fit.* They will honor all requests until their supply becomes exhausted—so act promptly!

3. When making a request, be certain to *print* your name and address clearly—and be certain to include your *zip code.* (If your zip code is missing, chances are your request will not be filled.) Be sure, too, that you have copied the name and address of the company making the free offer *exactly* as listed. Remember to request the item you want with the *exact* title specified in the order. And, as a rule, allow approximately 4 weeks for delivery.

4. Some firms, to facilitate handling, ask that you send your request on a postal card. (This is particularly true of many government offers.) Please respect their wishes. And make certain that your name, address, and zip appear on the *blank side* of the card. If they are written on the upper left-hand corner of the side with the stamp, very often the post office's cancellation marks will obliterate your address, making it impossible for the recipient to decipher.

5. *Please respect certain special conditions which may be stipulated.* If a stamped, self-addressed envelope is required, send one, with a 20¢ stamp attached. In the case of some unusually bulky items, 50¢ in coin may be asked for. If a *long* envelope is requested (known as a #10), please accommodate the sponsor. If the condition states that you must be a teacher, businessman, or member of a community organization to qualify for the free material, use your official stationery to prove your eligibility.

6. *Notice about handling charges!* Readers will notice that we are including a *limited number* of offers which call for a nominal charge for handling, packaging, and postage. These costs range from 25¢ to 50¢. We have examined the products accompanied by these stipulations and can assure you that in each case the nominal charge is well justified. Inflation and rising costs have put the squeeze on many of our sponsors. They still want to give you something valuable free, so show them some consideration by helping to absorb their handling costs. Notice, too, that even our most generous host, Uncle Sam, is this year requesting that you compensate him for the cost of mailing and handling. Please honor all such requests, or your order will be ignored!

7. Please do not write me or the publishers. It is impossible for us to handle such a vast correspondence. We can neither act as intermediary in seeing that you receive the items you want, nor can we assume responsibility that they will be sent to you. We can only repeat that everyone involved in this project is acting in good faith, and that legitimate complaints have been rare.

8. Please do not use the sources in this book indiscriminately. *Send for only the items you can really use.* It costs businessmen millions of dollars annually to offer the public free goods and services. You can show your appreciation by using their offers wisely.

9. *Beware of imitations.* From time to time unauthorized versions of this book appear on newsstands. Most of their offers are brazenly pirated from previous editions of this book and list items which are no longer in supply. 1001 VALUABLE THINGS YOU CAN GET FREE is the original and oldest compilation in this field, the most respected, with almost 4 million satisfied readers. Now turn the pages and learn how every day can be Christmas!

MORT WEISINGER

1

FOUR-STAR SUPERSPECIALS

Browse through this chapter before you buy this book—we guarantee that any three items you send away for will more than justify the price. We have estimated that it will cost the sponsors of the free albums, books, calendars, guides, maps, and magazines listed in this section alone more than half a million dollars to supply all the requests. And remember: These are just a few SAMPLES of the fantastic free gifts that await you in the following chapters.

Free Property Recorder

Have vital information about your valuables at your fingertips by recording this information in the New Jersey Council on Crime Victim's *Property Recorder*. The handy recorder, which measures a convenient 9½" x 5½", has space to record serial numbers, police identification numbers, color, size, make, model, and other essential information that you might need in the event that one of your valuables is lost or stolen. For the free *Property Recorder*, write to: Robert Grayson, Crime Victim Advocate, City Hall Annex, Paterson, N.J. 07505.

Birdwatcher's Picture Handbook

How many of the 800 species of birds in North America can you identify? The famous naturalist Roger Tory

Peterson has assembled a gallery of paintings which will enable you to recognize on sight the more than 100 live birds you can find in our fields and woods and at our seashores. And whether the bird is a sora, bufflehead, grackle, scaup, or killdeer, you'll be able to tell if it wades, swims, climbs trees, wags its tail, takes off from the water like a helicopter or like a seaplane. For your free copy of *Birdwatching*, write to: National Wildlife Federation, Dept. 001, 1412 16th St., NW, Washington, D.C. 20036.

Free Flag Brochure

An attractive brochure, *Our Nation's Flags*, which presents the national and 50 state flags in their true, glorious colors, is yours for the asking. Old Glory and our 50 state flags are illustrated, along with a brief commentary on the history of each. This publication is presented as a public service by the State Mutual Life Assurance Company of America. Write (postcard preferred): Dept. PR-B, State Mutual of America, 440 Lincoln St., Worcester, Mass. 01605.

The Freebie That's Bigger Than Texas

Here it is, readers, the most fabulous, most sensational giveaway ever offered in *all* twelve editions of this book! It's a blockbuster of an item (it weighs over 1 pound!) that's almost as big as Texas. Actually, it *does* come from the good people of Texas. It's a lavishly illustrated tour of the great Panhandle state, told in rich living colors, that goes on and on and on and on for 160 pages! Printed on coated paper, with a beautifully drawn cover painting entitled "Old Stagecoach of the Plains," drawn by the famous artist Frederic Remington. *Texas, Live the Legend* is the name of this giant geographical giveaway that brings to life the Alamo, the Astrodome, the NASA space center, and vacation attractions you never dreamed of! Free from: Texas Tourist Development Agency, Box 12008, Dept. MW, Austin, Tex. 78711.

Album of Classic Antiques

Here is a 40-page picture gallery of classic American furniture pieces, as selected by Marvin D. Schwartz, lecturer-consultant for the Metropolitan Museum of Art in New York City and columnist for *The New York Times*. The abundant photographs feature rare beds, chairs, cabinets, and desks which are on display in our country's leading museums. They illustrate each period in American craftsmanship. Not only is this handsomely produced album a joy to behold, but the author's running commentary will enable you to tell whether a piece of furniture is Duncan Phyfe, to see the difference between William and Mary and Queen Anne designs, to recognize the Shaker influence in home decor. The makers of Johnson Wax are the angels who produced this distinguished album, and you can get your free copy by writing to: Consumer Services Center, Dept. AF, Johnson Wax, P.O. Box 567, Racine, Wis. 53403.

VALUABLE CALENDARS

Free Date Book

A valuable "Date Book," containing a reminder file of dates and events, gift guides, calendars, mail rates, and Plan-a-Party checklists, is yours for the asking. It also carries information about anniversary and birthday customs. Your free copy awaits you at any place where Hallmark Cards are sold.

Tree Calendar

"Color It Green With Trees" is a permanent 12-month calendar guide for beautifying your yard or garden with the right trees. Spring and fall sections offer planting tips, summer section gives how-to-water information, winter section tells how to prevent snow damage. To obtain, send 50¢ to cover mailing cost to: Superintendent of Documents, U.S. Government Printing Office, Washington, D.C. 20402, and request the tree calendar #001-000-01557-5.

Baseball Calendar

The major league teams which train in Florida will play more than 160 exhibition games in the Sunshine State. For a free schedule of all games (from mid-March through early April), write to: Visitor Inquiry Section, Florida Division of Tourism, Room 402, Collins Blvd., Tallahassee, Fla. 32304.

GREAT GUIDES

Poker Possibilities

If you are one of the millions of Americans who enjoy an occasional game of poker, you can improve your luck by knowing the odds. A vest-pocket-sized chart lists your mathematical chances for drawing a flush, straight, etc., depending on your hand. To obtain, send a stamped, self-addressed envelope to: United States Playing Card Co., Cincinnati, Ohio 45212.

Prescription Guide

Dr. David A. Scheiman describes how a physician's prescription is translated to a pharmacist's label. Listed are common prescription symbols and their meanings, also how to care for drugs and where to store them. Obtain free by calling any local Quality Care office or sending a stamped self-addressed envelope to: "Understanding Your Doctor's Prescription," Quality Care, Inc., 65 Roosevelt Ave., Valley Stream, N.Y. 11580.

Learn How to Canoe

Learn the basics of canoeing on the best types of courses available. Organizations nearest you can help you find the best spots for canoeing, which are listed in this directory. For happy paddling write for a free copy of *Canoe Directory* to: Grumman Boats, Marathon, N.Y. 13803.

For Football Fans

Free . . . a special issue of America's leading gridiron weekly, *The Football News,* complete with predictions by the experts for both college and pro football. Write: The Football News, Dept. MW, 17820 East Warren, Detroit, Mich. 48224. Please include 50¢ for mailing costs.

U-HAUL Moving Guide

Moving doesn't have to be expensive. Move it yourself and save 75% by renting a U-HAUL trailer or 50% with a U-HAUL truck. This free 24-page booklet, in color, gives packing, loading, and storage tips and explains how to figure cubic feet for each room of furniture. Follow the guide's instructions and your books, chests of drawers, tables, and lamps won't "shake, rattle, or roll." The *U-HAUL Moving Guide* is yours free by writing to: U-HAUL International, P.O. Box 21502, Phoenix, Ariz. 85036.

Want to Be a Professional Bartender?

Even if you don't intend to work a bar professionally, the information in this book can be of great value when preparing drinks for your friends at home. There is no mystery in preparing drinks, but there are fundamental rules for perfect drinks. What kinds of glassware should be kept on your bar? For setups you should have which mixers, juices, bitters, garnishes, wines, liquors, and liqueurs? Learn how to make a Moscow Mule or a Brandy Alexander. Speed tips to make you a good bartender and the DON'TS that will bring reorders and bigger tips. Upon study and completion of the *Bartender Course* in this 38-page colored book, you will receive an original free certificate in two colors on simulated parchment, 8" x 10" and suitable for framing. For free booklet, *Bartender Course,* write to: Seagram Distillers Co., Box 1624 F.D.R. Station, Dept. JS, New York, N.Y. 10022.

Author, Author!

Do you dream of being a published author and seeing your by-line in print in a book or magazine, or under your story, article, or poem? The current issue of *Writer's Digest,* the leading writer's magazine, is yours for the asking. It offers information on hundreds of markets open to beginners and contains tips on writing by successful freelancers and editors. Send requests to: Writer's Digest, Dept. WBS, 9933 Alliance Rd., Cincinnati, Ohio 45242. Please enclose 25¢ for mailing and handling. (Regular price per copy is $1.)

Freelancer's Newsletter

Trying to place the things you write? *Freelancer's Market Newsletter* will keep you in touch with up-to-date leads on what magazine and book editors are looking for. To receive a sample copy, send #10, self-addressed envelope to: Freelancer's Market, 20 Waterside Plaza, New York, N.Y. 10010.

Newsletter for Medal Collectors

Art Medalist is a free newsletter for collectors of medals, published six times a year. Features news and information on medal collecting, medallic sculptors, editorials, pictures of new and historic medals. For a free subscription, send your request to: Editor, Art Medalist, c/o, Medallic Art Co., Old Ridgebury Rd., Danbury, Conn. 06810. After you receive your first copy, you'll want to award him a medal.

Silent Trail User's Wilderness Code

Be a good trailblazer on your next backpackers' trip. Learn safety and courtesy rules and how to be a good housekeeper in the forest. For a copy of *Silent Trail User's Wilderness Code* and a list of *Trail Guides,* send stamped, self-addressed envelope to: International Backpackers' Association, P.O. Box 85, Lincoln Center, Maine 04458.

Basketball Weekly

Yours for the asking . . . a sample copy of the publication *Basketball Weekly,* the national periodical that covers news of the pro and college basketball worlds. Lists schedules of games, ratings of players, and other statistics. For a copy, send 50¢ for postage and handling to: Basketball Weekly, Dept. MW, 17820 East Warren, Detroit, Mich. 48224.

For Chess Fans

For news of what's doing in the world of chess, a free copy of the publication *Check Us Out* is yours for the asking. Send requests to: U. S. Chess Federation, 186 Rt. 9W, New Windsor, N. Y. 12550.

For Better Investing

Do you have a sound approach to investing? Here's a magazine, third largest in circulation among financial magazines, which presents articles on growth stocks, professional analysis of companies and industries, market studies, and many aids for individual investors. In addition, you'll find specific companies for study, portfolio analysis, and proven stock selection guides. Send for a sample issue of *Better Investing,* monthly magazine of the National Association of Investment Clubs. Write: NAIC, P.O. Box 220, Royal Oak, Mich. 48068.

THE JACKPOT FOR JUNIOR

Kiddie Cookbook

Your small fry can learn to ride the range with *The Young Cook's Bake-a-Bread Book.* Teaches the kids, via a series of cartoons and rhymes, how to bake fresh bread. ("First of all . . . prepare your tools; that's one of the first baking rules.") Also features interesting historical facts about the staff of life. To obtain, send a stamped, self-addressed, *long* envelope to: Fleischmann's Yeast, P.O. Box 509, Dept. MW, Madison Square Sta., New York, N.Y. 10010.

Kiddie Craftbook

Develop your child's creative expression through simple craft projects with Play Clay. A color booklet, *Move Over, Michelangelo,* tells how kids can fashion jewelry, toys, decorations, vases, candlesticks, and pendant necklaces. It's stimulating, and they'll enjoy concocting the Play Clay out of pantry ingredients, baking soda, cornstarch, and water. For your free copy, send a *long,* self-addressed, stamped envelope to: Church & Dwight Co., Dept. PC, 2 Pennsylvania Plaza, New York, N.Y. 10001.

Kiddie Coloring Book

What better way to instruct your children about energy and using it wisely than through an educational coloring book? *The Energy Ant* explains in simple terms what energy is and where it comes from. In addition to the crayon coloring fun, there are words to unscramble, dots to connect, riddles, puzzles, cutouts, a trip to the moon, and even an energy-card game. Send your request to: Consumer Information Center, Dept. 640F, Pueblo, Colo. 81009.

Let the Animals Talk to Your Kids

Good Food News for Kids is a package of four illustrated booklets that introduces the basic food groups to your children. *Meet Fred the Horse Who Likes Bread* explains how bread gets from the farmer's field to your toaster. Fred tells what's so great about bread. And there's *Gussie Goose*, who introduces the fruit and vegetable group; *Mary Mutton*, who teaches your children about meat; and *Molly Moo*, natch, who pushes dairy products. Not only do these booklets discourage your kids from eating junk food, but they feature interesting puzzles. Write: Consumer Information Center, Dept. 525G, Pueblo, Colo. 81009.

The Story of Checks

Interested in orienting your children to the world of checks? A cartoon-type booklet, *The Story of Checks*, depicts in colorful panels the origin of checks, how checks are processed, and how we are likely to make payments in the future. Also included is a glossary of everyday financial terms related to checks which are easy for Junior to master. Write: Public Information Dept., Federal Reserve Bank of New York, 33 Liberty St., New York, N.Y. 10045.

SURPRISE GRAB BAG

The Name Game

What do the following have in common: cardinal, gray squirrel, pine, dogwood, honeybee, channel bass? Give up? They are, respectively, the official bird, mammal, tree, flower, insect, and fish of the state of North Carolina! Which state claims the mistletoe? Whose choice is the dragonfly? Which is the "coyote" state? Which *five* states have each selected the mockingbird as their official bird? You'll find the 300 choices of all our 50 states in an informative chart, "Official Birds, Mammals, Trees, Flowers, Insects, and Fish of the States." Free from: National Wildlife Federation, Dept. 001, 1412 16th St. NW, Washington, D.C. 20036.

Free EMI Card

Do you suffer from diabetes or epilepsy? Do you take any heart drugs? Do you wear contact lenses? Do you have any dangerous allergies? Carry an Emergency Medical Identification card on which you can record medical information. If you are not able to tell your medical story after an accident or sudden illness, the information entered on this card will speak for you. To obtain this wallet-sized free card write: Metropolitan Life, Health and Safety Education Div., 1 Madison Ave., New York, N.Y. 10010.

Jojoba—A Whale of a Bean

Grow Jojoba and help save the whales. Jojoba is a plant that produces beans that contain oil that is similar to sperm whale oil. If the world could produce enough Jojoba beans, there would never again be a need to kill the whales. Jojoba oil is used in makeup, motor oil, lubricating oils, shampoo, and hair oils plus other products. To obtain free Jojoba seeds send $1.00 for postage and handling to: KSA Jojoba, 19025 Parthenia St. #200, Dept. FT, Northridge, Calif. 91324.

2

GROOVY GIVEAWAYS FOR TEENAGERS

Kids, do we have goodies for you! Student travel tips. Clever ideas for making money in your spare time. And some valuable collegiate specials!

Color Her Beautiful

The swingy blonde and the bright brunette always seem to catch the eyes of the boys. And it doesn't matter to the guys whether the color was natural good fortune or if it came from a bottle or a tube. Did you know that more than half the teenage girls in the U.S. (more than 7 million) use a hair-coloring product? For information on how to tint your tresses, secrets of shampoo treatment for your hair, how to care best for your hair, whether it's long, curly or straight, oily or dry, and comb and dryer tips, send for the illustrated booklet *The Gentle Touch for Your Hair*. Free from: Park Packaging, P.O. Box 58, North Brunswick, N.J. 08902.

Congratulations! You're Growing Up!

What happens sometime between the ages of 9 and 16? When you first start to menstruate, it's natural to think about it a lot. You feel unique and different, and you know you've reached some sort of turning point in your life. This book discusses physical changes that occur

when you start menstruating, what is a normal period, the
sanitary products scene, dos and don'ts while menstruating, and medication to relieve discomfort. To receive this
24-page booklet with glossary free plus a free Midol
sample, send 50¢ for postage and handling with your
name and address to: Midol Booklet, P.O. Box 100, Murray Hill Station, New York, N.Y. 10016.

Insurance for the Graduate

Car insurance is the number one type of insurance
most graduates will need. You owe it to yourself to understand how it works, how it can protect you from personal
injury or property damage lawsuits every time you sit
behind the wheel. Besides, you and friends riding in your
car need protection against accidents involving uninsured
motorists. For excellent tips on buying your first policy,
send for the 20-page booklet *Getting the Most for Your
Insurance Dollar*. Write to: Communications and Public
Affairs Dept., D-1, Kemper Insurance Cos., Long Grove,
Ill. 60049.

Free Movie Stills

Gals—is your brother or an uncle stationed overseas?
If so, here's how he can get a free photo still of his
favorite actress to pin up in his barracks, provided she's
appearing in a movie produced by Columbia Pictures. Just
tell him to send a request to: Publicity Dept., Columbia
Pictures Corp., 1438 N. Gower St., Hollywood, Calif. 90028.
If he has an APO number, they'll honor his request. But
don't mention this offer to your boyfriend. He's liable to
ditch you for some screen siren!

What Are Your Chances for College Admission?

Are you concerned about the changes in college admission policies? This booklet, *A New Era In Admissions*, is
an examination of the changes in college admission policies, the declining enrollments, the role of standardized
testing, and possible supplementary methods of screening
applicants. For a free copy of *FOCUS 7*, write to: FOCUS7,
Room P–168, Educational Testing Service, Princeton, N.J.
08541.

For College-bound Coeds

Know a girl thinking about college? A flyer issued by four women's colleges in Virginia outlines a four-campus tour that takes in many points of historic and scenic interest in the Blue Ridge Mountain country. The Appalachian Trail and Blue Ridge Parkway, Monticello, Appomattox, and Natural Bridge can also be seen on a circular tour that covers Hollins, Mary Baldwin, Randolph-Macon Woman's, and Sweet Briar colleges, with the flyer showing locations of other nearby vacation attractions. With gasoline supplies a major question mark, girls taking the four-campus tour can combine a vacation with the all-important visit so helpful—and necessary—for choosing a college. For a copy of your *Four-College Campus Tour,* send requests to: Office of Information Service, Randolph-Macon Woman's College, Lynchburg, Va. 24503.

Are You Interested in Science?

Who sponsors science project work and what makes a good project? How can you be creative and think scientifically? Pointers you should know on gadgetry and planning, on collecting materials and choosing your field. Where to get sources of project ideas, information, and advice. Your exhibit may win an award at the National Science Fair. For a free bulletin, *Your Science Project,* write to: Edmund Scientific Co., 7782 Edscorp Bldg., Barrington, N.J. 08007.

Vision in Sports

"You can't hit it if you can't see it" is a saying often heard on the baseball diamond. If you can't see it, you also can't stroke, kick, bowl, catch, cast, aim, shoot, or drive it—depending on the sport. Don't scoff if we tell you your eyes don't have it. One optometric examination of more than 500 athletes in college revealed that 105 of the players needed visual corrections to improve blurred vision and reaction time. Give your eyes a break by sending for the booklet *You Can't Hit It . . . If You can't See It.* To obtain free copy, send a stamped, self-addressed envelope to: Communications Division, American Optometric Association, 243 North Lindbergh Blvd., St. Louis, Mo. 63141.

Be a Mermaid

Young girls from 18 to 25 looking for a full-time career can qualify for one of the most exciting careers of the day—Professional Mermaid! The famous Spring of Live Mermaids, Weeki Wachee, in Florida, is an underwater fairyland of beautiful live mermaids, exotic scenery, and millions of gallons of crystal-clear water. The girls perform daily for over 1½ million visitors a year, and Weeki Wachee is constantly seeking young girls who can learn the underwater acro-ballet routines to join one of the aquatic teams. To qualify, a girl must be athletic, graceful, and have no fear of the water. Surprisingly, she needn't be an expert swimmer! For more information, write to: Mermaid Supervisor, City of Live Mermaids, Weeki Wachee, Fla. 33512.

Fire Prevention Perky Posters

Famous personalities throughout history, including a few who got burned, stress the theme of fire prevention in colorful 8½ x 11½-inch posters. Available to individuals and organizations with a common concern for fire prevention, both on-the-job and in-the-home. NOTE: Parents, teachers, and other adults are advised in advance that the posters are sponsored by a segment of the tobacco industry and may be inappropriate for children. To obtain a free set, send 50¢ to: Smokeless Tobacco Council, Box 70, Peekskill, N.Y. 10566.

Cash In on Cans

Want to make easy pin money in your spare time and at the same time help the ecology? Then join the Great Aluminum Can Hunt. Yes, the Aluminum Association wants all the discarded aluminum cans you can gather— there are billions of empties—and will pay you about 15¢ a pound for your efforts. Last year can collectors, mainly teenagers, earned over $13 million in such spare-time scavenging! Some kids make about $14 to $20 a day scooping up the cans at beach parties and in picnic areas. Of course, the used cans are recycled, and the metal is conserved. To obtain a free copy of the *Aluminum Can Center Directory*, which lists the locations of hundreds of centers in the U.S. which redeem old cans, write: Aluminum Association, 750 Third Ave., New York, N.Y. 10017.

Which Career Would You Like?

These free booklets deal with both the wide range of jobs that are open to young people and the process of choosing a career. Choose your favorite—*Communications, Construction, Health Care,* or the *Arts* plus others. You can receive a series of 10 career booklets, by writing to: Careers, New York Life Insurance Co., Box 51, Madison Sq. Sta., New York, N.Y. 10010.

Trips for Teenagers

Teenagers, if you enjoy off-the-beaten-track travel, if your budget requires you to watch your dimes and dollars, a hosteling vacation is for you. American Youth Hostels, a nonprofit organization, offers information about budget travel in 50 countries for students, youth groups, fraternities, sororities, etc. Also tips on year-round travel in this country—hiking, biking, canoeing, and sailing with hostelers from your own local area. For a travel folder and other free literature, send a stamped, self-addressed, *long* envelope to: American Youth Hostels, National Campus, Delplane, Va. 22025.

For Tomorrow's College Students

The jump from high school to college is still a big one—and many a freshman is likely to find himself saying "I wish I'd known that *before* I came to college" some time during his first year on campus. With this in mind, the University of Rochester has culled its freshman classes for their most helpful tips for tomorrow's college students. Their published findings represent a scholastic gold mine for high-school students, parents, and educators. To obtain, send a stamped, self-addressed #10 envelope to:

Wish I'd Known, Office of University Communications, University of Rochester, Rochester, N.Y. 14627.

Student Travel Catalog

This is the "how-to" travel handbook for the academic community. Covers every aspect of inter- and intra-continental travel. Air and rail accommodations, work-abroad programs, unique tours, budget accommodations, trip insurance, and special travel documents. For free copy, send 75¢ for postage and handling to: CIEE Student Travel Service, 205 E. 42nd St., New York, N.Y. 10017.

Collegiate Special

A free service bulletin, *Hints on Summertime "College Prospecting,"* offers tips to teenagers and their families on how to visit your prospective college during vacation. Prepared by the admissions office of the University of Rochester, this bulletin gives suggestions for arranging an interview with the admissions counselor, clothes to wear on campus, etc. Requests must be accompanied by a stamped, self-addressed envelope and should be sent to: Dept. JB, Office of University Communications, University of Rochester, Rochester, N.Y. 14627.

Conn Brass Catalog

Interested in playing music with a group or a band? A new, full-color, 24-page catalog introduces you to the complete line of famous Conn brass instruments. The free catalog tells all about Conn trumpets, cornets, flugelhorns, euphoniums, baritone horns, tubas, sousaphones, recording basses, and saxophones. A special introductory section for each instrument illustrates and explains the design and manufacturing processes that produce the instrument's important features. Those who want to learn about brasses can write for the free booklet to: C. G. Conn, 616 Enterprise Dr., Oak Brook, Ill. 60521.

Baby-sitter's Bible

Want to be the best baby-sitter in town? Study the dos and don'ts in a helpful publication, *When Teenagers Take*

Care of Children. Let your neighbors know you've read this guide, and they'll beat a path to your door requesting your services. Free from: U.S. Dept. of Health, Education, and Welfare, Office of Child Development, 30 C Street, SW, South Building, G-024, Washington, D.C. 20201.

BritRail Travel SeaPass

In addition to the SeaPass, BritRail offers unlimited rail travel, one-way or round-trip travel, from London to the continental port by train and Sealink or Seaspeed and, in the case of Ireland, the addition will be one-way or round-trip travel from London to the Irish port by train and Sealink. For more information, write: BritRail Travel International, 630 Third Ave., New York, N.Y. 10017.

Dig This Jazz Guide

The Basic Record Library of Jazz is a selective list of especially important recordings that reflect the various styles and musical innovations in the history of jazz. The list is arranged by decades covering the 1920s through the 1970s. Contains approximately 250 recordings including many selections by best-selling, long-established jazz artists like Miles Davis, John Coltrane, Charlie Parker, Billie Holiday, Duke Ellington, and Louis Armstrong as well as major new artists like McCoy Tyner, Chick Corea, and John McLaughlin. Each section includes a brief historical introduction. Artists' listings are comprehensively cross-referenced. To obtain a copy, send a stamped, self-addressed, *long* envelope and 50¢ to: Schwann Jazz Catalog, Dept. 1001, 137 Newbury St., Boston, Mass. 02116.

Beautify Your Bedroom

A place to study or just to sleep, a haven for relaxation or visits with friends, a retreat for quiet hours of reading or thinking—that's what a bedroom can be. Why not decorate it to suit your life-style and personal tastes? Decorating need not be expensive and it can be fun. An idea-crammed booklet, *How to Redecorate Your Room,* teems with illustrated suggestions how you can brighten your room with wall hangings, curtain tricks, bedcoverings, lighting techniques, even clever wastebaskets. To obtain the booklet, write to: Consumer Services Center, Dept. H, Johnson Wax, P.O. Box 567, Racine, Wis. 53403.

Know-how With a Moped

Read about the "Big 5 of Moped Safety" before you zip down the street on your new friend or share the road with other mopedalists. Safety is the key word for Moped pleasure, for yourself and riders who depend on the driver. To obtain free colored brochure, send stamped, self-addressed, business-size envelope to: Moped Safety, 1001 Conn. Ave., NW, #707, Washington, D.C. 20036.

Freelancer's Newsletter

This is published twice monthly for professional freelancers-writers, editors, photographers, and illustrators. Includes information on new magazines as well as reports, news, and announcements of interest to freelancers and publishers. If you'd like a free sample copy, send a self-addressed, stamped envelope to: Freelancer's Newsletter, 307 Westlake Dr., Austin, Tex. 78746.

3

FREE BEAUTY AND FASHION AIDS

Ever since Eve, it has been a woman's world. So this book would hardly be complete without a special chapter devoted exclusively to the fairer sex. Males who peek in on the free loot for ladies listed here needn't turn green-eyed. Just turn to Chapter 16, "It's a Man's World."

Your Face Is Your Fortune

Many things are taken at "face value" . . . and that includes your *face*. What can you do to improve the way others perceive you? Take care of your skin. A new booklet, *You and Your Face Value*, helps you learn about your skin and how to treat it. The booklet answers many of the perplexing questions teenagers have about acne problems, and it delves into some of the common misconceptions on how to cleanse and care for the skin. For a free copy, send a *long*, stamped, self-addressed envelope to: You and Your Face Value, Sea Breeze Laboratories, Dept. V-78, P.O. Box 15598, Pittsburgh, Pa. 15244.

The Shampoo Story

Depending on your ability to remember shampoo brand names, you can have hair that can't tangle or tousle, hair with body, smoothness, sheen, luster, highlights, fragrance, and manageability, locks that stay locked come

hail, high wind, or humidity. But which shampoo to choose?
Can one shampoo product perform several cosmetic func-
tions as well as after-shampoo rinses? Is there anything to
be gained by buying an "egg" shampoo, or is it just an
advertising come-on? For the hard-core facts, read the
objective government report, *And Now a Word About Your
Shampoo*. Free from: Consumer Information Center, Dept.
573G, Pueblo, Colo. 81009.

Want a Facelift to Give You a Lift?

This comprehensive guide discusses various types of
cosmetic surgery. Included are typically asked questions
with easy to understand answers, plus an in-depth outline
of what each procedure entails, patient's preparation prior
to surgery, and recommendations following surgery. For
free brochure, write to: Drs. Steven Herman & Elliot
Jacobs, 800B Fifth Ave., New York, N.Y. 10021.

How to Care for Your Hair

What would the beautiful Rapunzel have done without her long golden locks? Think how different the story
of Samson might have been had Delilah not cut his strength-
producing hair. History, fairy tales, folklore, and biblical
stories relay the significance of hair and its appearance.
For a basic hair products list, special hair pointers, and
good advice write for this free 18-page, 11 x 8½-inch
booklet, *Hair Care*, to: Consumer Services Center, Personal Care Division, 1525 Howe St., Racine, Wis. 53403.

Attention Women!

Where can you go for counseling, advice on educational and work opportunities? Catalyst offers a list of 150
local resource centers and 50 free publications you can
request by writing to: Catalyst, 14 E. 60th Street, New
York, N.Y. 10022.

4

PARADISE FOR PARENTS

Do you know how to answer your daughter's questions about sex? What is the best way to give baby his bath? What to do if your kid is on drugs? How to figure out a weekly allowance for your children. You'll find all these vital child-care problems discussed in the following pages. More importantly, you'll discover how to solve them via a wealth of incredible giveaways. Literally, this chapter is a giant jackpot for Junior!

Parents Guide to Immunization

Do you know what immunization means? For which seven childhood diseases should your child be immunized? What side effects and after-care should every parent know about? This free 25-page immunization guide also includes an immunization record. For a copy of *Parent's Guide to Childhood Immunization*, write: Public Documents Distribution Center, No. 522G, Pueblo, Colo. 81009.

Raising Children

Children between the ages of 1 and 12 are in the formative years when parents must decide what to do about minibikes, TV programs, junk foods, permissiveness, and an occasional poisonous house plant. Raising youngsters safely and sanely is described in a new booklet, *Child-*

hood, which tells what parents should do, including how to raise a child's IQ, the special problems working mothers face, and what to say when a parent dies or divorces. This new, 96-page, illustrated health education booklet is available free from your local Blue Cross Plan.

Be Nutritionally Alert

There's a new wind blowing in medicine. Prevention is what it's all about. Good nutrition in the young years safeguards your health as you grow older. This booklet tells you nutrition facts you should know. For copy, write: Eating Well, Dept. EW-1001, Box 307, Coventry, Conn. 06238.

Child Safety

The booklet *Tips on Child Safety* describes ways to establish safety awareness in children, tips on poison prevention, and a guide to safe use of medicines and household products, according to Dr. Herbert S. Hurwitz, noted pediatrician. To obtain, send a long, self-addressed, stamped envelope to: Ms. C. Klein, Child Safety, 11th Floor, 300 E. 44th St., New York, N.Y. 10017.

Guide to Infant Skin Care

Babies get and deserve a lot of compliments. From birth your baby will be the object of love and adoration—from relatives, friends, neighbors, even strangers. You will share the credit with Mother Nature for baby's clear eyes, silky hair, and smooth skin. This booklet tells you the proper way to bathe and dry a baby, and about problems you can solve, such as diaper rash, chafing, prickly heat, and cradle cap, and problems that need a doctor's advice and care. For a free copy of *Infant Skin Care,* send your name and address plus 25¢ for postage and handling to: DeRidder/Thurston Inc., Att: Joe O'Heaney, Rochester, N.Y., 14610.

Make Baby Feeding Safe Feeding

This is an informative brochure with tips to insure happy and safe mealtimes for your infant. The pamphlet outlines important points about the best environment for feeding and for proper serving and storage of prepared baby food. For free copy, send a stamped, self-addressed, business size envelope to: Make Baby Feeding Safe Feeding, Closure Information Bureau, 300 E. 44th St., New York, N.Y. 10017.

Care and Safety of Children

This 12-page booklet is illustrated by Dr. Jay M. Arena, former president of the American Academy of Pediatrics. It offers timely advice on problems such as how toddlers can be protected from toxic household chemicals and how to teach children to understand the meaning of danger. For a free single copy, write for: "The Care And Safety Of Children", Council on Family Health, 633 Third Ave., New York, N.Y. 10017.

Tips on Child Safety

A must for parents, this pamphlet was prepared in consultation with a leading pediatrician to help prevent accidents among children. It covers poison prevention, guidance in the safe use of and storage information about child-resistant caps. For free copy, send a stamped, self-addressed, business size envelope to: Tips On Child Safety, Closure Information Bureau, 300 E. 44th St., New York, N.Y. 10017.

For Consumer Information on Toys

Four educational pamphlets are available to help you choose proper toys for your child. They are *Choosing Toys for Children, Parents Are the First Playmates, Toys Are Teaching Tools,* and *Playing Safely with Toys.* Available as a complete set of four only. Single sets can be obtained free of charge. To obtain send self-addressed, 31¢ stamped envelope to: Consumer Affairs Manager, Toy Manufacturers of America, Inc., 200 Fifth Ave., New York, N.Y. 10010.

Be a Better Santa

Ten toy tips for buying your children's toys. As you come down the chimney, be a smiling Santa with safe surprises. For free booklet, write: "How To Be a Better Santa Claus," Schaper Toys, P.O. Box 1230, Minneapolis, Minn. 55440.

How to Interest Your Child in Music

Interested in improving your day-to-day relationship with your child? Try music. A thoughtful booklet, *How Music Can Bring You Closer to Your Child*, not only describes the many merits of a musical-instrument education for children but answers many of the negative reasons parents give for not starting their children on musical instruction. Prepared by the manufacturers and the distributors of Leblanc (Paris), Noblet, Normandy, Vito, Holton, and Martin band instruments, it answers such objections as: "My child has no talent" . . . "My child shows no interest in music." Write to: G. Leblanc Corp., 7019 30th Ave., Kenosha, Wis. 53141.

Toys for Toddler to Preschooler

The right toys to help develop your child physically, mentally, and socially. Toys that can be hugged, squeezed, pushed, pulled, grabbed, rolled, shaken, tossed, banged, chewed on, and crawled after improve muscular skills. For the preschooler, magnetic spelling board, U.S. map puzzle, and play clock improve mental skills. For free colored booklet, *Toys for Toddler to Preschooler*, send a stamped, self-addressed envelope to Playskool, Inc., Dept. G.S., 4501 W. Augusta Blvd., Chicago, Ill. 60651.

The Playmobil Primer

Stimulate imagination and education with these series of lesson plans. For little people aged 4 and up, these knights, cowboys, Indians, construction workers, medical personnel, cavalry, and firefighters are part of a series which can be used in classrooms and home. Social studies and science concepts are two of many subjects you can seek. For this interesting free pamphlet, *The Playmobil Primer*, write to: The Playmobil Primer, c/o Schaper Toys, P.O. Box 1230, Minneapolis, Minn. 55440.

Before Choosing a Private School

How to Choose a Private School raises all the questions and provides many answers for parents who are considering the enrollment of their child in a private school. How can you judge the school's faculty? . . . Can a school be judged on the basis of cost? . . . How many graduates go on to college? There are elements, too, that a parent has to consider about the child's career goals, as well as the philosophy, standards, and capabilities of the intended school. Written by the headmaster of a prestigious 20-year-old private school, this booklet also provides a handy checklist that tells you at a glance what the public should know about private schools. To obtain, send a *long*, stamped, self-addressed envelope to: Highland School, 172-79 Highland Ave., Jamaica Estates, N.Y. 11432.

Junior's First Eye Exam

As your youngster approaches the time for that first visit to your optometrist (and a thorough examination at the age of 3 is recommended—earlier if there is any indication of a visual problem), a few practical suggestions will help you to ensure his cooperating with the doctor and enjoying this important first-time experience. For example, plan for an appointment early in the day, before the child is tired. Also, it is *extremely* important that you do not mention to your child the possibility of your child needing glasses. For vital information on how to prepare your child for this occasion, carefully read *Your Child's First Vision Examination*. To obtain, send a stamped, self-addressed envelope to: Communications Division, American Optometric Association, 243 North Lindbergh Blvd., St. Louis, Mo. 63141.

Drug Abuse

Your kids shouldn't know less about drugs than you do. A federal source book gives answers to the most frequently asked questions about drug abuse. Study it, then talk with your kids. To obtain, write to: Questions & Answers, National Clearinghouse for Drug Abuse Information, Box 1080, Washington, D.C. 20013.

Summer Programs . . . Which One Shall It Be?

The Advisory Council of Camps will help you select a suitable summer program that meets needs of your child. For free brochure write: School and College Advisory Center, 400 Madison Ave., New York, N.Y. 10017.

Free Birth-O-Gram Sample Cards for Expecting Parents

Get free samples of unique birth announcements that tie in with your work, sport, or hobby interests. Designs include auto, airplane, banker, dental, engineer, football, hunting, tennis, motorcycle, legal, music, salesman, teaching, twins, and many, many more. For your free samples—available to expectant parents only—state your work, sport, or hobby interests and expecting date. For 68-page catalog picturing 140 different original cards enclose 25¢ for mailing. Write to: Birth-O-Gram Co., Dept. 30, Coral Gables, Fla. 33134.

Now Hear This

Doctor, Is My Baby Deaf? is a useful booklet which explains signs that may indicate a hearing loss in babies aged 3 to 24 months, and what to do if those signs appear. Also available is a pack of materials which contains varied information concerning early detection and treatment of hearing loss in children. Introduction is by TV's Dr. Marcus Welby, the famous Robert Young. Order from: "Hearing Alert!" Alexander Graham Bell Assn. for the Deaf, 3417 Volta Pl., NW, Washington, D.C. 20007.

Children's Money Guide

An excellent "oracle" on money management for youngsters is this 32-page illustrated booklet, *Children's Spending*, a guide which is used extensively by youth counselors, clergymen of all denominations, and school educators. It discusses such problems as: "Should money be used as a disciplinary measure?" "What if a child loses his money?" "What if a child breaks something in the house, or breaks a neighbor's window?" "What if a child becomes envious?" "What if a child wants something very expensive?" "At what age should an allowance start?" "How often should an allowance be reviewed?" There is also a chapter on how to give a child experience in handling money. To obtain a free copy of *Children's Spending*, send 50¢ in coins, to cover mailing and handling costs, and write to: Money Management Institute of Household Finance Corp., Dept. VTF, 2700 Sanders Rd., Prospect Heights, Ill. 60070.

Play It Safe

A valuable safety catalog which features products to help protect young children from accidents is now available. It includes many carefully selected inventions for safety in every stage of child growth, from infancy through teenage. The catalog offers clever protective devices to guard against danger from electrical outlets, falls and cuts, fire, car accidents, and playground perils. Concerned parents who browse through the pages of *Child Safety Catalog* will be amazed by the ingenuity of the "Edisons" of the safety sector in perfecting lifesaving products. Free from: Safety Now Co., P.O. Drawer 567, Jenkintown, Pa. 19046.

5

LOOT FOR YOUR LIBRARY

Those with an eye for entertaining and instructive reading will be glad to know they can obtain free reading matter for their personal libraries, libraries that include science, unusual industrial sidelights, community affairs, and many valuable self-help booklets.

This literary bonanza is the gift of promotion-minded leading American companies. These firms put out a dazzling array of booklets, brochures, fact sheets, and pamphlets on every subject from art to zoology.

Now, let's zero in on just where you can collect this material to build a fine library that will bring you much pleasure as well as stimulation.

Bargain Books on American History

Interested in American history? Then here's an easy way to build up an expensive library of books on the subject. Simply send a postal card to: Superintendent of Documents, U.S. Government Printing Office, Washington, D.C. 20402, and ask to be put on their mailing list to receive their regular bulletin, *Selected List of U.S. Government Publications*. It will be sent to you, free, every 2 weeks and contains news of the latest books and publications printed by Uncle Sam, many of them devoted to phases of Americana, all offered at bargain, nonprofit prices.

Free Civil Liberties Quiz

If, like all good Americans, you believe in the Constitution and the Bill of Rights, how do you feel they should be interpreted in tense, difficult times like these? The nonpolitical, nonpartisan American Civil Liberties Union will send you its *Twenty Questions on Civil Liberties* and a list of its 60-odd pamphlets and publications—without charge. Ideal for controversial discussion and debates in high school classes. To obtain, send a stamped, self-addressed envelope to: American Civil Liberties Union, 22 E. 40th St., New York, N.Y. 10016.

Human Relations

Interested in obtaining low-cost (a nickel or a dime) literature concerned with overcoming bigotry and improving man's understanding of his fellow man? The American Jewish Committee has prepared a massive catalog, *Publications,* which lists the material available. Subjects include human relations, prejudice, mental health, and family life. This catalog is a wonderful resource for civic organizations, churches, synagogues, and schools. For a copy, send 75¢ in coins plus a *long* stamped, self-addressed envelope to: Publications Catalog, American Jewish Committee, 165 E. 56th St., New York, N.Y. 10022.

The Miracle of Rubber

A 23-page history of rubber from ancient times to today's moon age is offered by Goodyear, the world's largest tire and rubber company. Well illustrated, the booklet traces the discovery of natural rubber (some 2600 years ago), the eventual need for an invention of synthetic rubber, and discusses the astounding range of today's products that would not be possible without this miraculous material. Write to: Public Relations Dept., Goodyear Tire and Rubber Co., Akron, Ohio 44316.

How Children Grow

If science is your bag, send away for this special—*How Children Grow.* Its theme is based on the fact that the

mature human body is the end result of a growth process
that requires almost two decades for completion. During
this 20-year period, the individual who was the product of
two germ cells becomes an adult made up of over 100
trillion cells. But how does this miraculous process take
place? This new 56-page booklet, which explains this biological miracle, is the story of discoveries about human
growth by medical scientists at 80 general clinical research
centers. Write: Science and Health Reports, Div. of Research Resources, National Institutes of Health, Bethesda,
Md. 20014.

The Conquest of Insects

Did you know that there are more than 850,000 species of insects? Many insects help man—distributing pollen
among flowering plants, spinning silk, providing honey,
devouring other insects harmful to man. Others carry
disease, destroy crops and property. Destroying all insects
would not only be impossible, but foolish. But which ones
should man fight and which ones protect? And when the
line is drawn, how does man go about controlling insects
without damaging the environment and upsetting the del-
icate balance of nature? *The Conquest of Insects Harmful to
Man and His Possessions,* a colorful, profusely illustrated
brochure, published as part of the Gold Crest pest control
program, provides insight into some of these questions.
Free from: Insects, 341 E. Ohio St., Chicago, Ill. 60611.

The Story of Fermentation

This 20-page color booklet, *The Story of Fermentation,*
deals with one of the most momentous and far-reaching of
all scientific achievements: the ability to harness microscopic
living creatures in the service of mankind. It reveals the
wonders of fermentation chemistry and biochemical engineering, developed by scientists and skilled technicians in
industrial, governmental, and university laboratories here
and abroad, and shows how billions of microbes are now at
work in industry, producing substances that give us better
food and drink, better clothing and shelter, better medicine.
Great material for a science report. Write to: Pfizer, Public
Affairs Div., 235 E. 42nd St., New York, N.Y. 10017.

Research Advances

Science students—would you like highly original research material for a biology term paper? A fully documented government report, *Research Advances in Human Transplantation,* discusses the progress of U.S. General Clinical Research Centers and their programs in transplantation research. Covers kidney transplantation, heart, liver, lung, bone marrow, and even cross-species transplantation (use of animal organs for human transplantation). For your free copy, write to: Science and Health Reports, Div. of Research Resources, National Institutes of Health, Bethesda, Md. 20014.

Be Weather-wise

"Everybody talks about the weather, but nobody does anything about it," Charles Dudley Warner once remarked. Now someone *has* done something about it—Air France. In a fascinating, illustrated 16-page booklet, *What's the Weather,* they clue you in on early forecasting instruments, new scientific techniques, weather superstitions, and other related phases. The section on how jet pilots fly above the weather is most interesting. Also tells you how to understand such weather terms as *cumulus fractus, cirrus uncinus,* and *altocumulus undulatus.* To obtain, send requests to: Air France, Box 747, New York, N.Y. 10011.

The Wonders of Wood

Want to learn about wood in one easy lesson? About how it conserves energy and fuel, its environmental advantages, where it comes from, how much the United States now has, and how a lot more wood can be grown? You can, in a booklet entitled *Wood—the Renewable Resource.* The colorful, highly informative, and easy-to-read booklet explains that the timber supply shortages plaguing the country during recent home-building booms are artificial and avoidable, and that there are dozens of reasons why the United States should not run out of wood. Free from: National Forest Products Assn., 1619 Massachusetts Ave., NW, Washington, D.C. 20036.

You Can Make Money Talk

Everything about money—except free samples—is yours for the asking from the Federal Reserve. A series of booklets gives you unusual facts about coins and currency, tells how to detect bogus bills, how our Federal Reserve System works, etc. Great for a research project in an economics class. Titles include:

> *Counterfeit?*
> *The Federal Reserve System*
> *Fundamental Facts About U.S. Money*
> *Money: Master or Servant?*

To obtain any or all of these publications, send your request to: Federal Reserve Bank of Atlanta, 104 Marietta St., NW, Atlanta, Ga. 30303. Attention: Anne F. Chadwick, Asst. Manager, Research Dept. Money happy returns!

Energy Crisis Facts

A simple, easy-to-understand question-and-answer booklet, *The Energy Crisis,* explaining how it all started, how long it is likely to last, and what industry, government, and individual citizens can do to help reduce hardship and distribute available supplies fairly, has been prepared by the Institute of Human Relations, 165 E. 56th St., New York, N.Y. 10022. Single copies are available free on receipt of a stamped, self-addressed, *long* envelope.

Free Bible Studies Course

If your busy life is getting you down, or if you feel depressed and alone, you may want to spend some time evaluating the direction you are going. This guided study of the Bible can help you find the answers you are seeking. It has given many people new hope for the future. It has brought comfort to the sick and imprisoned. It has been a valuable aid to teachers and students. Its value is priceless, but you can receive it free. Each of the 4 large booklets in the course is mailed successively to you. Study at your leisure and return the exam. It will be corrected and returned to you with the next book. A certificate and another free book are awarded upon completion of the entire course. To enroll, write to: Bible Studies V4, Box 69, Wellsburg, Iowa 50680.

The Birth of Basketball

Every basketball fan will enjoy the little-known history of the origin of this great game in the illustrated booklet *Basketball Was Born Here*. It traces the invention of the game in December 1891 by Dr. James Naismith at Springfield College, Massachusetts. Did you know that in the very first basketball game, instead of hoops and nets, the baskets were half-bushel peach baskets, and that college janitors sat behind them perched on ladders to retrieve the ball after every score? The use of the peach baskets inspired the name of the game—basketball. Many other surprising facts, including the evolution of the rules, and a pictorial folder describing the Naismith Memorial Basketball Hall of Fame. To obtain, send a #10, self-addressed, stamped envelope to: National Basketball Hall of Fame, Box 175, Highland Sta., Springfield, Mass. 01109.

The Secrets of Nutrition

Millions of Americans aren't eating wisely. Not because they haven't enough to eat, but because they eat too many of the *wrong* things or too little of the right. In short: food is what you eat, nutrition is how your body uses food. If you aren't eating foods to meet your body needs you may be suffering from poor nutrition. Some of the damage caused may be irreversible. For example, what a young girl eats today may have an effect on the kind of pregnancy she will have years from now. What a pregnant mother eats may affect her child's growth and development. What a person eats—as an infant, a child, or an adult—can affect the length and quality of his or her life. To check on your eating habits, order the important booklet *Food Is More Than Just Something to Eat* from: Consumer Information Center, Dept. 562G, Pueblo, Colo. 81009.

The Story of the Tire

Here's a 16-page booklet, illustrated in color, that describes the discovery of natural rubber, Charles Goodyear's discovery of vulcanization, the development of synthetic rubber, the history of various tire cord fabrics, how a tire is made, and a description of the various types of tires on the road today. Free from: Public Relations Dept., Goodyear Tire & Rubber Co., Akron, Ohio 44316.

Free Flag Booklet

Do you know the rules for proper handling and display of the United States flag? A handy, pocket-size booklet, *Etiquette of the Stars and Stripes*, details the history and symbolism of our flag. It also explains and illustrates how to use and display the national emblem. The booklet gives the Pledge of Allegiance, all the words to the "Star-Spangled Banner," and the answers to questions asked most frequently concerning proper flag usage. For a single free copy, send a stamped, self-addressed envelope to: Americanism Director, Veterans of Foreign Wars National Headquarters, VFW Bldg., Kansas City, Mo. 64111.

The World's Eighth Wonder

Did you know that ships can be seen 40 miles out at sea from the top of the Empire State Building ... that visitors to its tower see snow and rain falling up ... and that the rain seen from that height is sometimes red? Fascinating facts and figures about one of the tallest buildings in the world are available in an illustrated brochure about this eighth wonder of the world. Invaluable for settling arguments. Also features a panoramic aerial map of New York City which pinpoints the 75 most important landmarks. For a free copy, write to: Observation Promotion Dept., Empire State Bldg., New York, N.Y. 10001.

Animals for Research

Today hundreds of thousands of people owe their health and their lives to medical research, much of which was initiated using laboratory animals. Since it is too dan-

gerous to administer a previously untried drug or attempt
an untested surgical operation on a human patient, medical scientists use animals like chimps and dogs, whose basic
life processes resemble man's, to make useful conclusions
about the effects of a new drug, surgery, or other therapy.
To learn the dramatic story of how our scientists work
humanely with these laboratory creatures, send for the
publication *Do We Care About Research Animals?* Free from:
Science and Health Reports, Div. of Research Resources,
National Institutes of Health, Bethesda, Md. 20014.

Free Science Catalog

Edmund Scientific Co. offers this $1.00 priced catalog
free. 162 pages of unique, bargain priced, and chipped
sets for science experimentors. Over 4,000 interesting and
fascinating products for hobbyists, school, and industry.
For a free catalog, write to: Edmund Scientific Co., 7782
Edscorp Bldg., Barrington, N.J. 08007.

FREE EDUCATIONAL BOOKLETS

1. *Let's Look at Leather* traces the uses of leather from
prehistoric days, when man clothed himself in animal skins,
to modern times, when an efficient pig-skinning machine
can remove pigs' hides at a rate of 400 her hour. Also
reveals the methods of tanning from the Indians' secrets
for tanning hides to the present-day tanning of leather
and the manufacturing of Hush Puppies casual shoes. For
a free copy, write to: Wolverine World Wide, Advertising
Dept., 9341 Courtland Dr., Rockford, Mich. 49351.

2. Science students looking for original material for
their term project will find pay dirt in a 28-page booklet,
Healers From the Sea. It presents the history of a research
achievement in the exciting new field of antibiotics, which
involved the scientists of three nations. Profusely illustrated
with microscopic close-ups. Free from: Eli Lilly and Co.,
Dept. TW, Indianapolis, Ind. 46206.

3. Junior can scoop his whole class with these offbeat
facts for his next science report. A government scientific
agency discusses active and ancient volcanoes, also contains photos and maps of their locations. For your free

copies of *Volcanoes* and *Volcanoes of the United States*, write to: U.S. Geological Survey, Visual Services, 800 18th St., NW, 6th Floor, Washington, D.C. 20242.

4. *Light and Man*, the dramatic story of light since the dawn of time. The visible light portion of the spectrum, the invention of the arc light by Sir Humphry Davy, Thomas A. Edison and the electric light, the fluorescent lamp, how an incandescent lamp operates, the mercury lamp. For a free copy, write to: GTE Sylvania Inc., Advertising Services Center, 70 Empire Dr., West Seneca, N.Y. 14224.

5. *Nonprescription Pain Relievers*, informative, authoritative booklet to assist consumers in deciding what pain reliever to buy. Provides results of research done on various pain relievers in terms of quality, reliability, and value. Write: Bayer Company, P.O. Box 159, New York, N.Y. 10016.

6. *Timber: World Resources and Reserves*. Can the earth's forests, totaling 12 trillion cubic feet of timber on 27% of the planet's land area, meet skyrocketing demands for wood throughout the world? How does the U.S. fit into the global timber supply picture? For an interesting booklet on this timely theme, write to: National Forest Products Association, 1619 Massachusetts Ave., NW, Washington, D.C. 20036.

7. *Air Traffic Control*. This 10-page brochure tells the story of air traffic control through an imaginary cross-country flight on the highways of the sky from takeoff to touchdown. Free from: U.S. Department of Transportation, Publications and Forms Section, TAD-443.1, Washington, D.C. 20590.

8. *Tips for Energy Savers*. "Don't be fuelish" is a popular slogan in these days of increased energy awareness; and saving energy in and around your home saves you money. This booklet offers suggestions for checking your insulation and other features that will guarantee you a warmer winter and a cooler summer. Free from: Consumer Information Center, Dept. 610, Pueblo, Colo. 81009.

9. *A Brief History of the Union Pacific Railroad*. The true saga of how engineers and men labored mightily to build the nation's first transcontinental rail line will keep you in suspense until the last spike is driven, the last rail is

laid. Illustrated with trestle and tunnel pictures. Free from: Union Pacific Railroad Co., Advertising Dept., 1416 Dodge St., Omaha, Nebr. 68179.

10. *It's Time We the People Spoke Up.* This is a public service message written by George Peppard, the famous motion-picture and TV star, which tells you how you can sound off on important issues to your congressman or senator by sending him a Personal Opinion telegram, at special economy rates. Lists the names of the senators in every state. Send requests to: Donn Dutcher, Public Affairs Dept., Western Union Corp., 1 Lake St., Upper Saddle River, N.J. 07458.

11. *Declaration of Independence and Opportunity for Older Americans.* Presented with a foreword by former President Ford, this booklet quotes him as saying: "Too often older and middle-aged people are the victims of myths and prejudices regarding their capabilities. We must give these men and women the chance to prove that time has only enhanced their abilities and that they have the skills and talents to pursue meaningful jobs or satisfying volunteer service." To implement these desires, a blue-ribbon panel of 17 leaders in business, education, industry, and other fields has established a National Center for Career Life Planning. Their declaration will interest all the 23 million Americans 65 years of age or over. For a free copy, write: National Center for Career Life Planning, American Management Assn., 135 W. 50th St., New York, N.Y. 10020.

12. *Wildlife Notes.* A fascinating collection of nature-oriented bulletins which discuss the unusual features of whales, polar bears, the bald eagle, the California condor, and birds of the big cities. Offers excellent research material. Free from: National Wildlife Federation, Dept. 001, 1412 16th St., NW, Washington, D.C. 20036.

AMERICANS FOR ENERGY INDEPENDENCE BOOKLETS

1. Farm to table: the food-energy link. From food production to food processing—how is energy used in food consumption, cooking, waste, and dishwashing? Read all about it in this excellent booklet, *Farm to Table: The Food-Energy Link.*

2. *Energy Conservation Imperatives:* How can we achieve energy conservation, and what are the problems? What are the conservation guidelines?

3. *U.S. Energy Resources & Needs:* If you're concerned about oil, gas, coal, uranium, and nuclear power, you'll find this booklet highly informative.

4. A series of 5 pamphlets with articles on the energy crises reprinted from *Reader's Digest* may be obtained for 25¢. Individual articles are 20¢ each. Write to: Americans for Energy Independence, 1250 Conn. Ave., NW, Suite 502, Washington, D.C. 20036.

6

FREE PAINTINGS, PICTURES, AND POSTERS

Stop, look, and listen if you want to know how you can get costly artwork, drawings, photographs, maps, colorful posters—free. Many of them are suitable for framing. These superb drawings and pictures can brighten up a child's room, the basement playroom, or your den. For classrooms they make attractive and educational bulletin board displays. You'll love them all.

Giant Map of the United States

A 31 x 19-inch color map of the United States, geographically accurate, is yours for the asking. The map shows hundreds of cities, rivers, national monuments, and parks, etc. An added feature is that it also shows how the famous Union Pacific Railroad System covers a 13-state area with 9500 miles of trackage. To obtain, write: Advertising Manager, Union Pacific Railroad Co., 1416 Dodge St., Omaha, Nebr. 68179.

Disney's Greatest Free Delights

They're favorites of stamp collectors and noncollectors of all ages. Seven big, beautiful, full-color postage stamps depicting characters from Walt Disney's most famous motion pictures—from seven different countries. Ideal for mounting in albums, charming framed wall hangings for children's rooms. For free stamps, send 50¢ for handling to: Bick International, P.O. Box 854, Van Nuys, Calif. 91408.

Free Pin-Up Photos of Movie Stars

Would you like an autographed, glossy photograph of your favorite movie star for your den or bureau? Famous movie idols like Sean Connery, Barbra Streisand, Jack Nicholson, and Dustin Hoffman will be happy to send you a personal photograph, autographed with their own signature, if you send them your request. Here's how:

First, watch the movie ads and note which motion picture studio has released the latest picture of the star you're interested in. Then write the star care of that studio, state that you are one of his or her fans, and ask for an autographed picture. (It won't hurt to include a rave about his latest movie.) Here are the names and addresses of the major studios: Twentieth-Century-Fox, Westwood, Calif. 90024; MGM, Culver City, Calif. 90230; Universal Studios, Universal City, Calif. 91608; Warner Brothers, Burbank, Calif. 91503; Paramount Films, Hollywood, Calif. 90028.

Note: a few stars of the "stingy set" may ask you to send 25¢ for handling and postage, but they are in the minority, usually five-time Oscar-losers.

FREE COLORING BOOKS

1. *Tuffy Talks About Medicine.* Presented in a format the size of *Time* magazine, this coloring book demonstrates the dangers of kids taking pills from the medicine chest without mother's guidance. Contains 14 pages of open cartoons on drawing paper, ready for crayon or paint brush. Send requests to: Audio Visual Services, P.R. & A., Aetna Life & Casualty, 151 Farmington Ave., Hartford, Conn. 06156.

2. *The Thing the Professor Forgot.* This coloring book emphasizes the importance of a well-balanced diet, but this time it's via pictures and rhyme. Professor Oonose Q. Eckwoose climbs onto the pantry shelf, finds his book behind a jar of jam, and observes: "If you're going to be

smart, be clever or shrewd, be sure to know there are four groups of food." Each food group has pictures for your child to color. Free from: Consumer Information Center, Dept. 527G, Pueblo, Colo. 81009.

3. *Children's Safety Lessons.* Help your children to learn the verses, sing the songs, and color the pictures in this 24-page booklet, and they will learn how to escape the hazards of being run over when crossing the street, playing ball, sleigh riding, flying a kite, etc. Teaches them ten lessons in all. Write: Communications & Public Affairs Dept., D-1, Kemper Insurance Cos., Long Grove, Ill. 60049.

4. *Children's Fire Safety Lessons.* This antifire coloring book uses clever rhymes and songs to warn kids about playing with matches and other fire perils. For example, it teaches them what to do if fire suddenly breaks out when they are alone at home. Write: Communications & Public Affairs Dept., D-1, Kemper Insurance Cos., Long Grove, Ill. 60049.

7

THE BIG HAUL FOR HOUSEWIVES

Despite today's push-button paradise, it seems that mother's work is never done. She still has to scrub floors, polish silverware, paint the woodwork, iron the kiddies' clothes, and what have you. So herewith a collection of free house aids which we consider the next best thing to a robot girl Friday.

Stain Dial

Hit the jackpot with a turn of the wheel. Special hints for removing special stains may help you save garments galore. Request *Stain Dial* from: Consumer Relations Dept., Box B, Texize Chemicals Co., P.O. Box 368, Greenville, S.C. 29602.

Free Hostess Tips

Nothing more thoroughly reveals your personality than the table you set. The Gorham Company, famed silversmiths since 1831, has prepared full-color brochures describing the *Total Tabletop* of Gorham Sterling, Gorham Fine China, and Gorham Crystal. For a free kit, write to: Gorham Co., P.O. Box 2823, Providence, R.I. 02907.

Dress Up Your Window Shades

An illustrated brochure, *Do-It-Yourself Ideas for Window Shades*, goes all out to stretch your decorating dollar!

It shows the many ways one can dress up a plain shade by trimming, appliquéing, or painting techniques. Suggested custom touches are illustrated throughout. It is chockful of "how-to" instructions for the handy—and also for those not so facile-fingered. The booklet is available by mail from: Window Shade Manufacturers Assn., Dept. MW, 230 Park Ave., New York, N.Y. 10017. Please enclose 35¢ to cover postage and handling.

Free "Fire Extinguisher"

You can make your own fire pail! Send for this bright red large label marked FIRE. Wrap it around an empty coffee can filled with baking soda and presto! . . . you'll have a handy fire extinguisher. Keep one within easy reach of your stove, and it will put out any sudden fire in moments. For your free label, plus other fire safety hints, send a self-addressed, stamped envelope to: Church & Dwight Co., Dept. F, 2 Pennsylvania Plaza, New York, N.Y. 10001.

Time-Saving Cleanup Tips

Mother never told you, but your vacuum cleaner will do many more chores for you than you are aware of. For instance, it will clean out accumulated dust from radiators and refrigerator evaporators in short order. It will also help restore the nap in carpet when dents from furniture legs appear. A 24-page booklet, *Everything You Always Wanted to Know About Your Home*, is the answer to today's domestic help shortage. It tells how to clean drawers and shelves, mattresses, closets, summer furniture, bamboo blinds, fireplaces, painted or wallpapered walls, leather and upholstered furniture—practically everything you can find in the Sears Roebuck catalog! Also contains a carpet-stain removal chart. To obtain, send a stamped, self-addressed, *long* envelope with 30¢ in stamps or coins to: Home Care Institute Library, Dept. CM, Bloomington, Ill. 61701.

Consumer Tips and Warnings

Making oldsters aware and wary of marketplace pitfalls and ripoffs is the purpose of *Your Retirement Consumer*

Guide, which offers practical information and dollar-saving advice on supermarket shopping, how to buy a new or used car, tips on buying a mobile home, funeral frauds, and ways of getting results when you have a consumer complaint. Write: NRTA-AARP, Box 2400, Long Beach, Calif. 90802.

Tricks for Super-Savers

Got the inflation blues? Then see if you can guess the *one* cheap substance that is so versatile you can use it as a dentifrice, a mouthwash, a foot soak, a relief for insect bites, burns, poison ivy, a personal deodorant, and a bath-water softener? Need some more clues? You can also use it to remove odors from the refrigerator, grease from kitchen utensils, clean and remove onion and garlic odors from wooden chopping boards. If you're still baffled, here's our final clue. You can also use it to alleviate occasional heartburn, sour stomach, or mild acid indigestion. This miracle substance is—baking soda, almost as cheap as dirt. For a helpful guide on how to use it in ways you never dreamed of, request a copy of *Baking Soda Around the House* from: Church & Dwight Co., Dept. E, 2 Pennsylvania Plaza, New York, N.Y. 10001. Enclose a *long,* stamped, self-addressed envelope.

When It's Your Move

The responsibility of a woman moving her family from a home long lived in to a new location always involves a mixture of happiness and sadness. It's usually the woman in the household who inherits the job of overseeing all the details of the move; in addition, she must be prepared to handle possible family emotional upsets. A kit containing five brochures suggests how women can deal with all the problems that may arise and how to get adjusted after the move. Included is a chart which will enable you to list a complete inventory of the furnishings and possessions in each of your rooms. To obtain this kit, request *A Moving Guide for the Home Manager* from: Atlas Van Lines Inc., 1212 St. George Rd., P.O. Box 509, Evansville, Ind. 47703.

Carpet Care Handbook

Carpets and rugs require special care regularly. A 32-page handbook tells what to do about such common problems as shedding, unraveling, mildew, fading, what can be done to restore crushed pile and curled corners, how moths and beetles in carpeting can be controlled, how to select the best carpet shampoo or spray foam cleaners, fiber facts you should know before purchasing your carpet. Also included is an index of more than 60 different stains, from alcohol, chewing gum, glue, and ink to mustard, nail polish, rust, syrup, and even *unknown stains!* Write to: Consumer Services Center, Dept. H, Johnson Wax, P.O. Box 567, Racine, Wis. 53403.

Laundry Lowdown

Do you know the best way to launder delicates, permanent press, regular fabrics, and woolen garments? Maytag makes it simple for you with an informative free brochure, *The Facts of Laundry*. All washable items in your home can be automatically laundered by choosing the correct recipe. Write to: Consumer Information Center, 181YG, Maytag Co., Newton, Iowa 50208.

Sample Polish Packet

Yours for the asking—a sample packet of Hagerty Silversmiths' Polish with tarnish preventive built in; enough to clean a small serving dish. For free packet, send stamped, self-addressed envelope to: W. J. Hagerty & Sons, Dept. 1001, P.O. Box 1496, South Bend, Ind. 46624.

8

EVERYTHING FOR YOUR HOUSE— ON THE HOUSE!

Do you know how to beautify your home with inexpensive lighting? How to spot invisible roof leaks before it's too late? How you can make your locks burglarproof? Whether you own a cottage or a castle, a bungalow or a mansion, on these next pages you'll find how every day can be Christmas for homeowners!

Creative Homemaking

Are crowded closets a problem in your home? Would you like to give your bathroom a new and different look at painless expense? Do you know how to prevent rust and corrosion in your outdoor equipment? What is the most efficient way to clean your kitchen exhaust fan? For a generous potpourri of all-around-the-house improvement and maintenance ideas, send for the useful booklet *Creative Homemaking*. Free from: Consumer Relations Dept., Box B, Texize Chemicals Co., P.O. Box 368, Greenville, S.C. 29602.

When It's Time to Reroof

When roofs were made of thatch or animal skins or mud, protection was all that we expected. Today, however, the roof has an additional function. It's an important decorative element in the design of a house. Color, style, and texture are important. Eventually a roof begins to age. Wind, rain, snow, and, most damaging of all, the sun take their toll. A new consumer *Guide to Roofing* is yours free by writing to: Certain-Teed Home Institute, P.O. Box 860, Valley Forge, Pa. 19482.

When Making That Apartment Move

Grab your hat and coat, pets and plants, but don't forget important details such as shutting off utilities and notifying credit card companies plus many other must-dos listed in *How to Make a Happy Move to Your New Apartment*. For free copy, write: Atlas Van Lines Inc., 1212 St. George Road, P.O. Box 509, Evansville, Ind. 47703.

Safety Tips From Safe Home Guide

How to protect your home and beat the burglar. How to fight a fire before it starts. Which are the best locks, fire extinguishers, and smoke detectors. Best place to keep a record of valuables. For free colored brochure, *Safe Home Guide*, write to: State Farm Insurance Co., One State Farm Plaza, E-8, Bloomington, Ill. 61701.

Roofing Magazine Tells All

Will a new roof help sell your home? What are your best roofing buys? What kind of styles are available in today's roofing shingles? Tips on everything from selecting the right color roof to thoughts on roofing and energy savings. If you're in the market for a new roof, write for a free copy of *Home Appreciation* magazine to: Certain-Teed Corp., P.O. Box 860, Valley Forge, Pa. 19482.

Home Maintenance

"A house is not a home," but it can be your castle with efficient housekeeping. Best methods for cleaning walls, ceilings, windows, kitchen and closet care, and insect control. For free booklet, *Home Care*, write to: Consumer Services, Golden Rondelle, 1525 Howe St., Racine, Wis. 53403

Paneling With Pizzazz

You're entitled to a little luxury. Surround yourself with the elegance and prestige of Georgia-Pacific paneling: hardwood for living room and library, softwood for TV room and bar, and milplank for bedroom offers country elegance at affordable prices. For your kitchen give your imagination full rein with budget Spectrum paneling. This colorful 31-page free booklet shows 20 lines of hardwood and softwood veneered paneling and woodgrain prints for homes, offices, and commercial interior as well as information on factory applied finishes, product specifications, installation and maintenance. For free catalog write to: Georgia-Pacific Corp., 900 SW Fifth Ave., Portland, Ore. 97204.

Do You Want to Remodel?

What's the first step? Should you do it yourself or hire professional help? Do heating, plumbing, and electrical jobs require an expert? Do you have the time, patience, skills, and tools to do a good job? Must you have a building permit? Is remodeling a good investment? What home improvements can you finance? Read all about it in this free Andersen booklet of answers. Get tips on popular remodeling projects from adding a dormer to a sundeck. Obtain the *Andersen Remodeling Answer Book,* by writing to: Andersen Corp., Dept. R, Bayport, Minn. 55003.

How to Panel a Room

From a bedroom to a basement you can do it yourself with this free 35 x 22-inch guide. 73 diagrams show construction practices from measuring to Masonite Paneling installation. Obtain free copy of *Masonite Paneling Guide* by writing to: Masonite Corp., 29 No. Wacker Drive, Chicago, Ill. 60606.

Deck Out Your House With a Deck

Few improvements will increase the value of your house as much as a deck. Camouflage backyard problems with bi-level deck; on chilly nights a deck with a fire pit will keep you warm and cozy. Included are recipes for your first deck party. For this free 32-page magazine in color write to: "Great Possibilities," Georgia-Pacific, 900 SW Fifth Ave., Portland, Ore. 97204.

Water, Water Everywhere

Water sports may be one of America's most popular outdoor activities. If, however, heavy rains mean you can stay home and paddle your canoe in the basement or water-ski across your lawn, you may not feel like being a sport about it. Unless you live in a rice paddy, what you have is a drainage problem. The cause can range from seasonal high water tables or springs and seeps to slow soil permeability. Sometimes natural drainage systems have been blocked or altered during construction causing run-off water to seek other routes—perhaps around and through your home. Some solutions include installations on individual properties or in neighborhoods; others call for community action. To help you dry out, send for the booklet, *Drainage Around Your Home*, which identifies some causes of drainage problems and offers solutions. Write: Information Div., Soil Conservation Service, U.S. Dept. of Agriculture, Washington, D.C. 20250.

Hi-Fi Hints

Before you invest in hi-fi equipment for your home, it would be *good* to know something about what high fidelity is all about. It would be *better* if you could learn some of the language used in high-fidelity reproduction. It would be *best* if you were able to read the manufacturer's specifications with some understanding. A free booklet, *High-Fidelity Sound*, discusses essentials: harmonic distortion, dispersion, dynamic range, frequency response, and other hi-fi highlights you should know about. Included is a hi-fi dictionary which defines such terms as "rumble," "wow," and "flutter." Free from: Hi-Fi Booklet, Koss Corp., 4129 N. Port Washington Ave., Milwaukee, Wis. 53212.

The Condominium Craze

Housing economists predict that 50% of the United States population will live in some sort of condominium housing within 20 years. Statistical trends support that prediction. If you are considering purchasing a condominium dwelling, bear in mind that it's a lot more complex than buying a house. First, you must understand the condominium concept, because when you live in a condominium, you share certain responsibilities with your fellow tenants. Don't dare sign any document without the advice of a knowledgeable lawyer. To help clarify the various problems so that you know the difference between a latent defect bond and a leasehold interest, study the booklet *Questions and Answers About Condominiums* so that you'll know what to ask before you buy. Write: Consumer Information Center, Dept. 602G, Pueblo, Colo. 81009.

City Survival Guides

Transplanting a family to a large, unfamiliar city can be a disheartening experience. The Bekins Company is making the uprooting and resettling process easier for its long-distance customers by publishing *Survival Guides*. Bekins, operator of the world's largest moving and storage company, has prepared comprehensive guides to 15 of America's largest cities in order to help new residents adapt.

Weather, housing costs, locations of hospitals, schools, local government office, tax rates, and employment opportunities are covered. Also listed are churches and synagogues, libraries and other cultural centers, social services; even sports, banking, and liquor laws are discussed. Guides are available for: Atlanta, Boston, Dallas-Fort Worth, Chicago, Denver, Houston, Los Angeles, Miami, New York, Philadelphia, Phoenix, San Diego, San Francisco, Seattle, and Washington, D.C. Phone your local Bekins agent for a guide.

For Veterans Only

The Veterans Administration has a new booklet which explains all areas of concern to veterans who are prospective home buyers. If you're a veteran of World War II, the Korean War, or have service after Jan. 31, 1955, your various GI loan rights are available until you use them, with no deadlines. For a free copy of *Home-Buying Veteran*, write: Consumer Information Center, Dept. 600G, Pueblo, Colo. 81009.

Water Riddle

What's filling but not fattening? What has no calories and cleanses inside as well as out? What is hard or soft, colorless, odorless, and weightless? What is man's life line and nature's prize? How often do you go to the tap to quench your thirst and find the water distasteful? In which of 5 classifications as designated by the Water Conditioning Foundation does your tap water fall? Answers are in this 60-page, illustrated, $1.00 paperback. Yours free by sending a self-addressed 6 x 9-inch envelope with 75¢ postage to: Water Quality Association, 477 E. Butterfield Rd., Lombard, Ill. 60148.

Keep Cool

Which air conditioner for you? With dozens of companies selling hundreds of different models with cooling capacity ratings ranging from 4000 to 30,000 British thermal units per hour, the choice can be a problem. Picking the wrong model can result in your wasting electricity. Be watt-wise! Before you visit the dealer, study the booklet *How to Choose the Room Air Conditioner Best Suited for You*. It also discusses various advantages of different types of conditioners which should influence your buying decision. Free from: Assn. of Home Appliance Manufacturers, 20 N. Wacker Dr., Chicago, Ill. 60606.

Mobile Homes, Anyone?

If you are wondering whether or not a mobile home will serve your needs as a first home, a retirement home, or vacation hideaway, an informative booklet, *Your Mobile Home Buying Guide*, zeroes in with the answers. The guide offers a factual analysis of mobile home living, discusses costs and taxes, what to look for in mobile home construction, and how to find a mobile home that fits your lifestyle. Also contains a checklist to help you determine your specific needs. Write: Wickes Homes, P.O. Box 97, Argos, Ind. 46501.

The ABC's of Windows and Doors

Panel doors, like fine furniture, have a dimensional look that brings character to a room or an entrance. Right from the entryway and throughout your home, doors give a strong impression of your lifestyle. There's a wide choice of different wood designs in doors and their uses: for entrances, between rooms, folding, sliding, and closet doors. To find out about doors you can adore, send for *Remodeling With Windows and Panel Doors.* Write: National Woodwork Manufacturers Assn., c/o SR&A, 355 Lexington Ave., New York, N.Y. 10017. Also included is a section on how to select the right kind and style of windows that will last the lifetime of your house and prevent heat loss.

TV or Not TV

Lieutenant Colombo is just about to exhibit the clue that betrayed the killer when suddenly your TV screen starts to look like a jigsaw puzzle. Don't throw a soda bottle at your set—just send for the illustrated booklet, *How to Improve Your TV and FM Reception.* Written in simple, nontechnical language, it explains the reasons for poor reception and tells how to correct the most common problems.

Written in Q & A format, it supplies the answers to such questions as: What causes "ghosts" and "snow," and how can they be eliminated? Does color TV require a special antenna? How can you pick up telecasts of blacked-out games? How do you strengthen weak signals? What should you know before buying a new antenna for your location? Should you hook up to a cable TV system? TV will stand for Terrific Viewing if you use this information. To obtain, send a stamped, self-addressed, *long* envelope to: Channel Master Div. of Avnet, Ellenville, N.Y. 12428.

Improve Your Ceilings

Ceilings do make a difference—in both the appearance and comfort of your home. You can choose an elegant acoustical ceiling, fissured or perforated to absorb disturbing household noises, a smartly styled decorative ceiling for the look of high fashion, an exciting embossed ceiling to add striking "sculptured" dimension, or a modern Suspended Ceiling System, with lay-in panels in acoustical or decorative styles. All are styled to highlight any room, will blend with modern or traditional furnishings, are washable for easy care, and easy to install. For your guide, *How to Install Ceilings*, specify Booklet IB-167 and write to: Johns-Manville, P.O. Box 1960, RP-B, Trenton, N.J. 08607.

A Shade for Every Window

Casement windows, double-hung windows, apartment windows, and door windows—they all call for special shades. Do you know what shade is for which window and the right way to install it? To clue you in, a comprehensive, illustrated booklet, *Window Shade Primer*, offers "shaded solutions" for the almost endless variety of window types and shapes featured in all types of homes. Also includes imaginative suggestions for original ways to use window shades, how to measure shades, and how to clean shades. To obtain, send 35¢ to cover cost and handling to: Window Shade Manufacturers Assn., Dept. MW, 230 Park Ave., New York, N.Y. 10017.

Solve Your Water Problems

Are you concerned about hard water, and do you know the simple way to detect it? Or is your water supply cloudy, bad tasting, or bad smelling? Worse, still, does your faucet spout water that contains iron, ruining the flavor of tea and coffee and staining plumbing fixtures and laundry? If you're beset with any of these problems, it makes good sense to send away for the free booklet *Tips on Water Conditioners*. Write to: Water Quality Assn., 477 E. Butterfield Rd., Lombard, Ill. 60148.

Antinoise Tips

Noise in the Home, a booklet which points out the growing hazards of noise pollution, is being offered by the Koss Corporation of Milwaukee, manufacturer of stereophones. Featuring a decibel counter of common household noises and suggestions on how to reduce their impact, the brochure is based on findings of a University of Wisconsin study. To obtain, write: Noise, Koss Corp., 4129 N. Port Washington Ave., Milwaukee, Wis. 53212.

Free Bathroom Ideas

Your bathroom is a very important place. It's the first place you go in the morning, and the last place at night. There are good reasons for making it a pleasant and comfortable place to be in and use. In planning for a new house, there are many things you can do about the sink, shower, tub, floor, and fixtures to make the bathroom functional and attractive. A booklet, *Imaginative Ways With Bathrooms*, brims with great ideas. Write: Consumer Information Center, Dept. 609F, Pueblo, Colo. 81009.

Light Book

Here's a definitive 40-page manual, *How to Be at Home with Lighting*, which illustrates the fantastic ways you can use lighting designs to make the colors in your home live—create a pleasant working environment in utility areas, create a cheerful welcome in entrance halls and foyers, give you ease of seeing into drawers and shallow closets, use reflected light from mirrors to beautify your bathroom, make reading in bed a relaxing pleasure via proper lighting to permit both eye comfort and body comfort. Let the experts show you how functional fixtures, planned light distribution, and simple shielding material can achieve these effects. For your copy, write: Nela Press, #1180, Dept. 102-4548, General Electric Co., Nela Park, Cleveland, Ohio 44112.

Title Tips

If you are considering buying a new house to meet the individual needs of your family, give thought to the fact that safe, sound, reliable title insurance is of major importance. It is a basic homeownership protection essential to the security of your home. To avoid legal booby traps in this vital but little-known area, study every enlightening line in the free booklet *31 Questions and Answers About Title Insurance.* Available from: Lawyers Title Insurance Corp., P.O. Box 27567, Richmond, Va. 23261.

Beat the Burglar

Burglaries are committed in the U.S. at the rate of more than one per minute. You can foil Mr. Raffles by making your home burglarproof. An illustrated booklet, *How to Protect Your Home and Family Against Burglary*, suggests tips, describes the latest locks and chains to guard against entry via windows, garage door, sliding glass doors, cellar, etc. Send requests to: Mr. William Tell Thomas, Marketing, Kwikset Div., Emhart Corp., 516 E. Santa Ana St., Anaheim, Calif. 92803.

Your Own Laundry Center

Having a convenient, efficient, and attractive laundry center in your home has always been desirable. An illustrated brochure, *A Primer of Home Laundry Planning*, shows in pictures how you can plan a laundry center in the bedroom-bath area, the kitchen area, a family room, a patio, breezeway, carport or garage, or the basement. Economy of space is considered in all these plans. You'll marvel at the ingenious suggestions for creating room for hampers, baskets, etc. And don't overlook the valuable tips on what to know about each appliance you buy. Free from: Consumer Information Center, Dept. 38YG, Maytag Co., Newton, Iowa 50208.

Tips on Airborne Insecticides

How to use them in the home against flies, mosquitoes, flying moths, wasps, and gnats. When and how to use airborne insecticides and precautions to take while using them. For free brochure, *Airborne Insecticides* write to: Consumer Services, Johnson Wax, Racine, Wis. 53403.

9

OWN A FREE HOBBY LOBBY

Everyone should have a favorite pastime or hobby. In this age of the 40-hour week, learning how to make the most of your leisure time can help to enrich your life. Pick the pastime that best suits your taste and purpose, and it will enable you to relax from the pressures of a busy life.

Every member of the family can participate in this wonderful world of hobbies. Parents and children can share such avocations as photography, model railroads, philately, and sculpture. Herewith our roundup of some of America's most popular pastimes and free offers which, we hope, will inspire you to take advantage of them!

Build Your Own Railroad

Those great-name trains, such as the 20th Century Limited, Golden State, and Chief, have not sunk completely into oblivion. Scale models of these famous streamliners make countless runs every year—across the basements of America. *Model Railroader* magazine estimates 250,000 Americans engage in model railroading. The hobby is worldwide, with domestic and foreign manufacturers supplying the equipment and accessories. A 32-page illustrated booklet, *Introduction to Scale Model Railroading*, tells how to get started in this fascinating hobby. For your free copy, write to: W. A. Akin, Jr., Model Railroader, 1027 N. 7th

St., Milwaukee, Wis. 53233, and pretty soon you'll find the fast limiteds highballing (in exact scale) over your basement or attic model railroad.

Model-Car Collector's Guide

Car buffs, young and old, will delight in this free "Matchbox" collector's catalog of precision-crafted scale models of modern and unique vehicles. The full-color 40-page booklet lists over 75 modern vehicles, from bulldozers to racing cars, plus over a dozen antique and classic models of yesteryear, and over 20 heavy-duty commercial models. All models are authentic and shown in full color, making a fine guide for experienced collectors, or a source of inspiration for beginners. For your free copy, write to: Lesney Products Corp., Dept. MW, 141 W. Commercial, Moonachie, N.J. 07074.

Fun With Bottles

Save those old bottles. Whether they used to contain shampoo, beer, ink, ketchup, medicine, or whatever, you can easily convert them into useful objects for the home. A 34-page illustrated guide offers suggestions for scores of bottle creations, ranging from an aquarium lamp to a musical bottle. You can become acquainted with this unique hobby by sending for the book *How to Make Useful Articles for the Home from Glass Bottles*. Write to: Glass Bottle Blowers Assn., AFL-CIO, 608 E. Baltimore Pike, P.O. Box 1069, Media, Pa. 19063. Enclose 50¢ to cover expense of mailing and handling.

Treats for Train Fans

If railroadiana is your thing, there's a treasure chest of fascinating train memorabilia available that can add real class to your collection. An illustrated catalog, *Santa Fe Gift Selections*, features such unique items as dining-car chimes, gold-finished railroad spikes you can use as paperweights, engineer hats, baggage stickers, trainmen buttons, bookends made from 1881 Krupprail, a souvenir belt buckle, a complete set of the last timetables for such famous trains as the Super Chief, El Capitan, San Francisco Chief, Texas Chief, and many other items. For your free catalog, write: Advertising Direction, 224 S. Michigan Ave., Chicago, Ill. 60604.

The ABC's of Skating

Everything you wanted to know about roller skating is contained in this illustrated guide, *How to Roller Skate & Have Fun*. A series of action cartoons shows you how to start and stroke, how to steer, how to stop, how to adjust your skates. There's a section on trick turns and spins showing you how to do the "Figure Eight" and the "Spread Eagle" turn, how to skate backward, and other fancy footwork on eight wheels. Also suggests several novel games to play on skates such as wood tag, tin-can rolling, and the hilarious Japanese tag. To obtain, send 40¢ for mailing and handling to: Chicago Roller Skate Co., 4458 W. Lake St., Chicago, Ill. 60624.

The Art of Archery

If you've ever envied the skill of America's thousands of William Tells who can score a bull's-eye with a bow and arrow, here's your chance to get on target. Ben Pearson, America's ace archery dealer, has prepared an illustrated brochure, *How to Shoot a Bow and Arrow*, which will teach you the seven basics: (1) string the bow; (2) nock the arrow; (3) stance; (4) draw; (5) anchor; (6) aim; (7) release. Also advises you how to select the correct arrow length, bow length, and bow weight, depending on your size. (Directions apply even if you're left-handed.) For your free copy, write to: Ben Pearson Archery, P.O. Box 270, Tulsa, Okla. 74101.

Make Your Own Menagerie

Wouldn't you like to make a bird house, whale bank, or bird feeder without it costing a sou? Don't discard empty bottles or empty trigger sprayers. Be crafty and inexpensively transform these throwaways into toys, dolls, and decorative accessories. Make a moosehead or mouse planter with empty containers, glue, bottlecaps, and paper.

For free brochure, write: Crafty Critters, Consumer Relations Dept., Box B, Texize Chemicals Co., P.O. Box 368, Greenville, S.C. 29602.

The Wonderful World of Fishing

Fishing is America's No. 1 sport, and is enjoyed by 60 million men, women, and children of all ages. Fishing is different from most sports: it has no rule book, boundary lines, time limits. Its only requirement is clean water in which fish can live. Fishing does have its own special equipment and skills. If you want to be introduced to this fascinating fun-for-the-family hobby and have access to streams, dams, waterfalls, cutaway banks, and lakes, an informative booklet, *How to Catch Fish in Fresh Water,* will get you off to a fly-casting start. If you live in coastal areas and must fish in surf waters, bays, oceans, and other briny spots, you'll need *How to Catch Fish in Salt Water.* Either of these booklets is available free from: Fishermen's Information Bureau, 20 N. Wacker Dr., Chicago, Ill. 60606.

Have a Hobby With a Microphone

What is the mystique about microphones? Dispel the mystery by reading this 15-page instructional guide with a step-by-step approach and simplified technical terms. Diagrams explain what a microphone is and how it works. Useful to amateur and professional recordists. This basic knowledge will improve quality of homemade recordings. For free copy of a *Guide to Microphones,* write to: Audio-Technica U.S., Inc., 33 Schiwassee Ave., Fairlawn, Ohio 44313.

Your "Hometown Main Street" Project

In a nationwide pilot project called "Main Street," the National Trust for Historic Preservation is trying to get decaying downtowns to preserve their own authentic character. This free fact sheet and *Main Street Newspaper* offers guidelines on how to preserve that hometown look and how to get federal or foundation money in the bargain. Project gives source ideas for planning, funding, and researching in *Main Street, A Preservation News Supplement* (dated May 1978). To get on the free mailing list, write to: National Trust for Historic Preservation, 407 S. Dearborn, Suite 710, Chicago, Ill. 60605.

Introductory Guide to Duplicate Bridge

More than 500,000 people in the U.S., Canada, and other parts of the world play duplicate bridge regularly, and the number is growing by leaps and bounds. What is the fascination of this game? What should you know about it before you sit down to your first game? How can you improve your score? A free guide put out by the American Contract Bridge League provides the answers. Included in the guide are explanations of the difference between duplicate and rubber bridge, some of the tactics and ethics of tournament competition, how players win master points and thus earn various ACBL rankings, how tournaments are organized. Also free on request is the annual *Directory of Affiliated Duplicate Bridge Clubs*, which lists some 5500 clubs throughout the continent that are sanctioned by the league, which permits the clubs to award master points. To obtain any of these booklets, write to: American Contract Bridge League, 2200 Democrat Rd., Memphis, Tenn. 38131. Happy Grand Slam!

For Comic Book Collectors

Did you know that an old Superman, Batman, or Captain Marvel comic book can fetch you $100? Comic book collecting has become a national hobby for young and old. If you'd like to start your collection, or purchase copies that are missing in your sets, a free price list featuring the titles of the various comic books and their issue numbers is available from a dealer who has more than one million comics from all publishers in stock. He also buys comics. If you are interested in selling any, send a list of the titles, numbers, and conditions of each issue along with your asking price for each book. To obtain a massive free list of Marvel's, DC's, etc., or to sell comics, send a long, stamped, self-addressed envelope to: Grand Book, Inc., Dept. F, 659 Grand Street, Brooklyn, N.Y. 11211. (A list cannot be sent unless you include the long, stamped, self-addressed envelope.)

Stamp Collectors

Fill empty spaces in your stamp album with this fantastic collection of 77 different U.S. stamps. This genuine collection of colorful stamps includes postage-dues, airmails, commemoratives, and old classics. All this is yours as a gift to introduce National Stamp Co.'s fine, low-priced U.S. approvals. You may buy only what you need and return the balance without obligation. Send 40¢ for postage and handling to: National Stamp Company, Dept. N, Box 18, Westbury, N.Y. 11590.

IF MUSIC IS YOUR HOBBY

Harmonica, Anyone?

Do you have an aptitude for music? The easiest self-starter for anyone who wants to express himself musically is the harmonica. Teach yourself to play this enjoyable instrument by sending for the beginner's booklet *How to Play the Hohner Harmonica*, written by the eminent musicologist Sigmund Spaeth. For free copy, send a self-addressed, stamped envelope to: M. Hohner, Dept. S, Hicksville, N.Y. 11902.

Free Record Library Guide

For the serious-minded record collector, particularly the beginner collector of classical music, here is a 16-page pamphlet of suggestions for building a record library of great music. Suggestions are listed by composers in the following musical eras: medieval and renaissance, baroque, classical, romantic, and 20th century. Includes 150 really basic compositions, together with approximately 1000 additional selections to help find more music you like in any given period. To obtain a copy, send a stamped, self-addressed, *long* envelope and 65¢ for handling to: Schwann Record Catalog, Dept. 1001, 137 Newbury St., Boston, Mass. 02116.

All About the Organ

The organ is fast becoming one of America's most popular musical instruments. For every two pianos sold to homeowners, an organ is sold. Unlike pianos, organs come in an extensive variety of sizes, with numerous variations in sounds, keyboards, tabs, and stops. If you are interested in purchasing one of these glorious instruments for your home, send for the free booklet *Selecting the Right Organ*. To obtain a copy, write to: Hammond Organ Co., Dept. TW, 4200 W. Diversey, Chicago, Ill. 60639.

The Parker Brothers Story

Do you enjoy playing parlor board games like "Monopoly," "Cluedo," and "Careers"? Then you may be interested in the fascinating story of the famous game manufacturer who pioneered these products—Parker Brothers. The unique story of their industry, *75 Years of Fun*, recounts the behind-the-scenes drama of the inventors who devised their popular games, discusses their psychological appeal to the public. This may be just what you need to inspire you to invent your own game. Who knows? To obtain a copy, write to: Parker Brothers, Salem, Mass. 01970.

Ricecraft

The craft-minded home decorator or gift-giver will enjoy these ingenious ideas using simple rice to make mosiacs, jewelry, and sachets. The 6-page leaflet also explains how to tint rice and form sculptures, candy dishes, and even topographical maps with a rice-and-glue mix. Write: Rice Council of America, P.O. Box 22802, Houston, Tex. 77027.

Great Stamp Giveaway

For beginners as well as sophisticated philatelists. A catalog illustrating special issue and Bicentennial commemorative covers, maxi-cards, etc., issued by the International Stamp Collectors Society. Packet includes "Stamp Expo" collectors program with full-color stamp series cover and free stamp collectors gift. Send 60¢ for postage and handling to: Bick International, 6253 Hollywood Blvd., Hollywood, Calif. 90028.

The Bonsai Bonanza

The ancient oriental art of bonsai culture—growing miniature trees in pots—is booming as a hobby in this country. With bonsai, it is possible to have a tree on your apartment balcony. The aim of bonsai culture is to develop a tiny tree that has all the elements—and illusion—of a large tree growing in a natural setting. A government booklet, *Growing Bonsai*, tells how to create a bonsai in just five seasons. The booklet describes the five basic styles of these lovely and exotic trees; lists trees, shrubs, and other woody plants suitable for your bonsai hobby; and gives tips on how to obtain plants, how to display your bonsai indoors and outside. To obtain, send 50¢ to cover mailing and request publication # 001-000-02772-7 from: Superintendent of Documents, U.S. Government Printing Office, Washington, D.C. 20402.

Make Your Own Gifts

Each of us has a special talent for making something. And everyone has special friends with special occasions that call for the handmade crafts which say, "Hey, you're special and I made this for you." An illustrated booklet, *A Raft of Craft Ideas*, will inspire you on how to make unique gifts from scraps, bits and pieces, and reusables for little or next to nothing. The tools required to make the gifts and items in this craft sampler are mostly found around the house. A real treasury of fun-ideas! Free from: Consumer Services Center, Dept. H, Johnson Wax, P.O. Box 567, Racine, Wis. 53403.

10

A SHOWER FOR THE BRIDE

Before you set that wedding date, it would be wise to send away for every item listed in this chapter and go over them with your fiancé. They represent a literal shower of useful gifts for the bride—none of them borrowed, nothing blue, a few of them old, most of them new. Happy wedding!

After the Courtship, Coffee

After the billing and cooing, hubby will savor a good cup of coffee. Learn the art of preparing the perfect cup by studying the directions in a guide, *All About Making Coffee*, guaranteed to satisfy the ex-bachelor. Free from: Pan-American Coffee Bureau, Consumer Information, Dept. 200, 1350 Ave. of the Americas, New York, N.Y. 10019.

Marry-Go-Round

The most hectic period in a girl's life is the time between her engagement and her wedding. To guide the prospective bride through these preparatory months, an invaluable booklet, *The Marry-Go-Round*, offers step-by-step tips. Covers info on attire, rings, invitations, and pertinent details of a formal wedding. For free copy, send 50¢ for postage and handling to: The Marry-Go-Round, Gingiss Formalwear, Dept. MW–10, 180 N. LaSalle, Chicago, Ill. 60601.

A Diamond Is Forever

Diamonds are a girl's best friend—but do you know how to get the best value for your dollar? What do you know about the "4Cs" in a diamond—color, clarity, cut, and carat? All these precious facts, plus information on how to care for a diamond, are discussed in a 34-page booklet. The history of the diamond and engagement ring also is included. Free from: Diamond Promotion, 260 W. Lehigh Ave., Dept. GH, Philadelphia, Pa. 19133.

Your First TV set

After the wedding you'll discover that the second most important piece of furniture in your house will be your TV set. You will depend on it daily for news, information, and entertainment. Because your set is such an important purchase, you should study the advice offered in *Tips on Television Sets*. Discusses color TV, screen size, remote control, antennas, and service policies. This pro-consumer booklet is available free if you send a *long*, self-addressed, stamped envelope to: Electronic Industries Assn., P.O. Box 19369, Washington, D.C. 20036.

Jiffy Meals

Newlywed working wives who want to impress the hungry male will bless the expert chef who concocted these dishes you can whip up in jiffy time. Tells how to make lunches, dinners, and TV snacks in minutes—as delicious as if you fussed for hours. The secret lies in knowing how to glorify pizza rolls with a variety of tangy sauces, converting them into cheese balls, dressing them up with mushrooms, olives, shrimps, and even lining 'em up on a skewer shish kebab style. For a copy of *10 Marvelous Meals in Minutes with Jeno's Pizza Rolls*, write: Jeno's, P.O. Box 6264, Duluth, Minn. 55806.

Two on the Isle

Looking for the perfect honeymoon spot? A perfect haven is Nassau/Paradise Island. A colorful honeymoon kit is available for bridal couples. It describes special packages to fit every budget. Write: Nassau/Paradise Island Promotion Board, 255 Alhambra Circle, Coral Gables, Fla. 33134.

The Lenox Line

Why keep your girlfriends in suspense about what you'd like for your shower? When they snoop around slyly trying to get a hint, don't be coy—give them a clue. Show them the pattern booklets on the complete lines of Lenox China, Lenox Crystal, Oxford Bone China, Temper-ware, and Lenox Cuisine. You can do your good deed by marking off the line you prefer on the free china/crystal pattern coordination guide that comes with this offer. And see the exciting new collection of Lenox China Jewelry—a selection of lovely gifts for any occasion. To obtain, write to: Ellen Lynch, Director, Women's Club Activities, Lenox, Old Princeton Pike, Lawrenceville, N.J. 08648.

His and Hers

Wives—have you discovered, to your chagrin, that your hubby drinks too much? Don't nag him. Simply send for a copy of *What Happened to Joe.* Told in comic-book style, it narrates the story of a young construction worker who couldn't resist the sauce. Remember—a picture is worth a thousand words—and this little lesson has plenty of pictures. (It's only fair to mention, as a service to husbands, and to prove we're not chauvinists, that if wifie imbibes to excess, a similar comic book for the fair sex is available, entitled, *It Happened to Alice.*) To obtain a copy of *Joe* or *Alice*, send 40¢ for each item to cover mailing and handling to: AA World Services, P.O. Box 459, Grand Central Sta., New York, N.Y. 10017.

When the Budget Is Limited

If you are buying furniture for your first apartment, if you need a piece of furniture for that empty corner in the living room—think "refinished." Prudent newlyweds who would rather build up a nest egg than live it up beyond their means would do well to study the tips in the free booklet *A Beginner's Guide to Refinishing Furniture.* By buying used tables, chairs, chests, and other furniture, and refinishing them yourself, you can save a great deal of money because refinishing supplies cost only a few dollars. Refinishing or "restoring" furniture increases beauty, utility, and life—and often the value. Also, it's fun and gratifying. For a free copy, write to: Consumer Services Center, Dept. H, Johnson Wax, P.O. Box 567, Racine, Wis. 53403.

Don't Be a Dummy

Have you avoided joining your husband in the popular game of bridge because the bidding system baffles you? For a crash course which tells you almost instantly how to evaluate the tricks in your hand, send for the mini-pamphlet *Point Count Bidding*. Study the easy-to-remember rules in this booklet, and hubby will never want to change partners! To obtain, send a stamped, self-addressed envelope to: United States Playing Card Co., Cincinnati, Ohio 45212.

Enjoy Yogurt

The honeymoon is over. You've quit your job and settled down to being a good housewife. And now that you have access to the fridge 24 hours a day, the chances are you'll be tempted to snack it up all the time. Then, before you can say devil cake, you'll lose those curves he married you for. So throw the devil a curve and stock up with yogurt. It's tasty and low-caloric, and can be served in a variety of yummy styles. Therefore, if you want the honeymoon *never* to be over, send for the booklet *Yogurt and You.* To obtain, send a stamped, self-addressed envelope to: Yogurt and You, Dannon Milk Products, 22-11 38th Ave., Long Island City, N.Y. 11101. (This offer limited to readers who reside east of the Mississippi.)

What You Should Know About Your Breasts

Questions women ask most about their breasts, including cosmetic surgery and the effects of pregnancy, weight gain or loss, and bralessness, are answered in a 14-page booklet. Choosing the right bra, the physical makeup of the breast, and self-examination of the breasts are also explained. Write: Jantzen, Dept. GH, 666 5th Ave., New York, N.Y. 10019.

Now That the Wedding Is Over

The newlyweds are at home now that the honeymoon is over. She keeps the house clean and cooks the meals. Right away she discovers that the shower and the wedding gifts do not include all the tools and utensils she needs for a convenient, well-equipped kitchen; and pronto, both she and he realize that "current expenditures" must cover food for two. Don't press the panic button. Help in stocking the kitchen and the pantry in keeping with your budget is available in a government booklet, *Food for the Young Couple*, #001-000-02851-1. To obtain, send 45¢ with your request to: Superintendent of Documents, U.S. Government Printing Office, Washington, D.C. 20402.

Selecting Your Diamond

Here is a fabulous offer—an immense 92-page full-color deluxe catalog of fine diamond jewelry. Printed on heavy-coated stock, this *Cosmopolitan*-sized catalog features between its covers one of the most exciting collections of fine jewelry ever assembled in one book ... exquisite creations of treasured gold set with diamonds, sapphires, rubies, emeralds, pearls ... the world's most precious gems. Thumb through its pages and you may find the one piece of jewelry you've always yearned for—at a price you never dreamed possible. To obtain, send 40¢ to cover postage to: Empire Diamond Corp., Dept. 1001, Empire State Bldg., 350 Fifth Ave., New York, N.Y. 10001.

Man-Pleasing Recipes

To serve frozen TV dinners—or to impress him with tasty, "he-man" dishes—that is the question. A colorful cookbook supplies you with recipes designed especially to get you off the hook and bring praise from the head of the household. *Man-Pleasing Recipes* offers a whole array of ways to add zest to menus from entree to dessert by utilizing versatile rice in combination with meats, seafoods, herbs, and vegetables. Booklet also lists imaginative serving suggestions which provide instant ways to dress up rice and create "rave" dishes, guaranteed to satisfy the heartiest appetite. To please the man in your life, send 35¢ to: Rice Council of America, P.O. Box 22802, Houston, Tex. 77027.

Before You Buy That First Carpet

About to spend some of your wedding gift cash for that first carpet? You know, of course, that your carpet covers the floor and is walked on constantly. It takes more punishment than any other decorative material in your home. So you can use expert advice on how to prolong the life of your carpet. An informative booklet, *How to Care for Your New Lees Carpets,* offers maintenance tips on vacuuming, stain removal, surface brightening, avoidance of shrinkage, and other "first-aid treatments." To obtain, write: Lees Carpets, King of Prussia, Pa. 19406.

11

DO-IT-YOURSELFER'S GOLD MINE

If you are a weekend carpenter, spare-time builder, amateur fence maker, or Sunday mechanic, here are a variety of projects that will give your workshop a super workout. Simply study these easy-to-follow plans which show you how to do it step by step.

Want to remodel the interior of your house? Insulate your home in one afternoon? Transform that open porch into a comfortable additional room?

Free Roof Instructions

Homeowners who have a yen to play the role of "fiddler on the roof" will find inspiration in the booklet *Roof and Wall Shingling Made Easy*. Step-by-step illustrations show safe, easy ways to apply a new roof or repair leaks by reroofing with ever-popular and reliable red cedar shingles. Free from: Red Cedar Shingle & Handsplit Shake Bureau, 5510 White Bldg., Seattle, Wash. 98101.

Build Your Own Desk-Workbench

Fathers, if you're looking for an ideal "dad-son" project, these free, comprehensive plans will show you how to construct a useful desk-workbench for Junior which will provide many years of service. With the lid down, the 26 x 48-inch top is a perfect place for him to spread out books and other materials during homework sessions. To transform the unit into a workbench, he simply lifts the top and snaps a hook into place. A deep trough for tools and supplies is located behind the workbench. To obtain, send a postal card to: Home Service Bureau, Marlite Paneling, P.O. Box 250, Dover, Ohio 44622. Ask for plan 103-B.

Patio Awning Plan

For cool enjoyment of outdoor living build a patio awning this summer. It's a lot easier than you think, particularly if you use translucent fiberglass Filon-Stripes. A free patio-planning kit and building plans also tell how you can build light-admitting fences and garden sheds. Yours for the asking from: Filon, 12333 S. Van Ness Ave., Hawthorne, Calif. 90250.

Recessed Wall Cabinets

Recessed wall cabinets can be used effectively in almost any room of the house. Ideas illustrated in a new do-it-yourself handyman plan will enable hubby or Junior to design and build practical units. Step-by-step diagrams show how to build standard wall cabinets. In addition, the plans show how to include niches, shelves, shadow boxes, and bookshelves in your home-improvement project. To obtain, send a postcard to: Handyman Plans, Marlite Planning, P.O. Box 250, Dover, Ohio 44622. Request plan 105.

Chain Saw Savvy

Strictly for the graduate do-it-yourselfer, *All About Using Chain Saws* discusses the merits and maintenance of the lightweight chain saw, invaluable to timber workers, farmers, and occasional woodcutters. Tells how to carve rail fences, bridges, log cabins, etc. Profusely illustrated. Write to: Advertising Dept., Oregon Chain, Omark, 9701 S.E. McLoughlin Blvd., Portland, Ore. 97222.

Pocket Partner

A new tool pocket catalog for pros and amateurs is yours for the asking. This 31-page illustrated catalog, ideally suited for quick reference on tools in the famous S-K line, fits handily in shirt or jacket pockets. Write: Tool Group, Dresser Industries, 3201 N. Wolf Rd., Franklin Park, Ill. 60131.

Build Your Own Wine Rack

A booklet, illustrating more than a dozen easy-to-build redwood wine rack plans, and complete with directions and material lists, is now available. In addition to plans ranging from simple tabletop models to larger bulk storage facilities, the booklet supplies design and construction ideas, various finishing suggestions, and tips for proper storage of your wines. There's a 65¢ charge for mailing and handling, but it's well worth it when you consider how you'll be preserving your expensive wines. Write: Redwood Wine Rack, Louisiana-Pacific Corp., 1300 S.W. 5th Ave., Portland, Ore. 97201.

Calling All Inventors

Breathes there a do-it-yourselfer who hasn't thought he's got as much on the ball as Rube Goldberg? If you have an idea for a new gimmick, remember that industry is always on the hunt for new products. Write for the free booklet *How to Safeguard, Develop, and Market Your Inventions to Industry*. This booklet outlines what steps an inventor must take to properly present his invention to manufacturers for cash and royalty sales. Write to: Lawrence Peska Associates, Dept. PA, 500 5th Ave., New York, N.Y. 10036.

Be Your Own Plumber

You'll be plumb pleased by this handy booklet, *You Can Save Water With a Fluidmaster Tune-Up*, which tells you how to pinpoint toilet maladies and how to repair them yourself—without having to pay a piratical plumber's bill. Tells how you can fix leaky flush valves, worn-out tank balls, flabby flappers, and noisy tanks. Free from: Fluidmaster, P.O. Box 4264, 1800 Via Burton, Anaheim, Calif. 92803.

Build Your Own Greenhouse

Almost every gardener eventually reaches a point where he decides his green thumb deserves a treat . . . a greenhouse all his own. Once the big decision is made to build a greenhouse, you'll have to consider how much time, money, and work the project will involve. A hobby greenhouse can range from a simple polyethylene-covered framework to a fully automated conservatory with many choices in between. A USDA booklet, *Building Hobby Greenhouses*, discusses best locations for greenhouses, basic types and their design and construction, and information on obtaining plans and drawings. There are sections on temperature, humidity, and light control. To obtain, request Publication #001-000-03692-1 and send $1.25 for mailing and handling to: Superintendent of Documents, U.S. Government Printing Office, Washington, D.C. 20402

For Fathers and Sons

Every son looks up to a dad who can show him how to build a boat, birdhouse, airplane, table, or toy out of a few pieces of wood and some glue. It's easy to be a wizard at woodwork projects if you send away for a free copy of *The Joy of Accomplishment.* Write to: Stanley Works, Advertising Services Dept. P.I.D., Box 1800, New Britain, Conn. 06050. Included is a chapter on selecting the proper tools for a home workshop, plus a variety of available patterns for building projects. Enjoy the pride on your son's face when he shows you a finished piece of work and says: "I made that myself!"

The "73 Picture" Guide

Would you like to convert a dingy basement into a dazzling den? You don't have to be a Handy Andy to do the job yourself with this "can't miss" guide, *How to Panel a Room.* A series of 73 sharp photos show, in consecutive action, every step you should take in tackling such a project, from measuring the length, width, and height of the area to be paneled, to the triumphant 73d step, a view of the finished wall with its rich, beautiful patterns. Free from: Masonite Inquiry Clerk, Dept. I, 1909 E. Cornell Dr., Peoria, Ill. 61614.

Four Free Decorating Brochures

Planning to beautify your home? Remodeling ideas and decorating suggestions to make beautiful things happen to major areas of the home can be found in a new series of four paneling idea brochures from Georgia-Pacific. Contents include full-color reproductions and descriptive product data for creative uses with 17 hardwood veneer paneling lines in a wide array of styles, colors, and textures. Paneled wall surfaces in living and dining rooms, kitchens and nooks, bedrooms and dressing rooms, and family rooms and dens are shown. For *Beautiful Walls Booklet,* send 50¢ to: R.E. Perdew, Georgia-Pacific Corp., 900 S.W. 5th Ave., Portland, Ore. 97204.

Home Insulation Guide

Are soaring bills for gas or oil heating raising your blood pressure and diminishing your bank account? Don't climb the walls. An illustrated 32-page booklet which outlines the cost-saving benefits of a fully insulated home is yours for the asking. Entitled *Everything You Ever Wanted to Know About Roofing, Siding, and Residential Insulation,* and authored by Mort Waters, editor of *Family Handyman,* it's a must for every homeowner. Using a question-and-answer format, this guide provides hundreds of useful tips on home maintenance, selecting contractors, making product selections, and do-it-yourself activities. Write: Certain-Teed Home Institute, P.O. Box 860, Valley Forge, Pa. 19482. Please enclose 35¢ for mailing and handling costs.

Do It Yourself With Wallpaper

What easy rules make hanging wallpaper a pleasure instead of a pain? How to plan your wall coverage with estimating chart. Methods to ready walls and remove old covering. Paste and place, and your redecorated room will have that new look. For a free brochure, write to: How to Hang Wallcoverings, Advertising Dept., Sherwin-Williams Co., 101 Prospect Ave. NW, Cleveland, Ohio 44115.

How to Choose a Roofer

This *Homeowner's Guide to the Selection of Quality Roofing* highlights types of roofs, coverings available, what's new in asphalt shingles, how to prepare for roof fire safety and wind resistance, clues that tell when a new roof is needed. Importance of color illustrated with chart and color schemes. Obtain free booklet by sending 50¢ for postage and handling to: Asphalt Roofing Manufacturers Association, Box 3248, Grand Central Station, New York, N.Y. 10017.

Pamper Your Pool

What is more refreshing than a swim in a clean clear pool? How to keep water sparkling, basic tests and chemistry rules. How to solve water problems and best time to chlorinate. For free booklet, *Guide to Swimming Pool Care*, write: Church & Dwight & Co., 2 Pennsylvania Plaza, New York, N.Y. 10001.

Kitchen and Bath Planning

How to get that dream kitchen or bath that you can afford. A place for everything in the kitchen and bathroom. To receive a free brochure of *Kitchen and Bath Planning*, send 50¢ with your name and address to: National Kitchen Cabinet Association, Dept. CM, P.O. Box 2987, Grand Central Station, New York, N.Y. 10017.

Before Your House Is on Fire and "Smoke Gets in Your Eyes"

Know early warning devices—how they work and where to locate detectors. Make an escape plan NOW. For information on smoke and fire, write to: Public Relations Dept., Aetna Life & Casualty, 151 Farmington Ave. Hartford, Conn. 06115.

What Is the "Silent Menace" Around Your House?

It lurks in many of the medicines and household products you bring into your house. While these substances are safe and effective when properly used, some are potent enough to cause injury when carelessly used. Throughout this booklet, you'll find tips to help you prevent your family from becoming victims of poisoning. Included are pull-out sheets that tell how to treat poisons if inhaled, poisons in eyes, and poisons on skin (chemical burns), and how to treat the symptoms of shock. The back of the booklet has an emergency label to stick to your telephone cradle. For a free copy, write to: Silent Menace in Your Home, National Safety Council, 444 N. Michigan Ave., Chicago, Ill. 60611.

Have a Rapport With Your Roofer

Break down the home maintenance "language barrier." Be knowledgeable. Save time and money on reroofing. Know the roofing terms that the roofer uses. For a free *Glossary of Roofing Terms*, write to: Certain-Teed Home Institute, P.O. Box 860, Valley Forge, Pa. 19482.

Save Money by Insulating Your Attic

Be warm when winter winds blow. Diagrams and instructions on easy do-it-yourself insulation. To obtain free brochure *Insulate Your Attic Now*, write: Certain-Teed Corp. P.O. Box 860, Valley Forge, Pa. 19482.

12

YOUR FREE GARDEN OF EDEN

Calling all home gardeners! Green thumb or not, we've got acres of free aids for you on everything horticultural. You'll bloom all over when you see how that powerful postcard can transpose your land into a Garden of Eden.

Free Garden Book

If you'd like to give your lawn, garden, or backyard patch that "planter's punch," send for the new giant annual edition of *Burpee Seeds and Everything for the Garden*— 180 pages, many in color, scores of illustrations! You'll find it a helpful guide to the best flower and vegetable varieties, house plants, fruits, berries, ornamentals, trees, vines, shrubs, roses, ground covers, and lawn grass; with planting tips on all. Write to: W. Atlee Burpee Co., Warminster, Pa. 18974; or Clinton, Iowa 52732; or Riverside, Calif. 92502. (Select address nearest your home.)

Greenhouse Plan

If you want a good home greenhouse at reasonable cost, build it yourself. It's easy and fun to do with Filon Home Greenhouse Panels—a line of fiberglass plastic sheets developed especially for hobbyists by the world's largest maker of greenhouse panels for the commercial greenhouse industry. Plans offer complete step-by-step instructions, shopping list, and cutting schedule. Free from: Filon, Dept. VT, 12333 Van Ness Ave., Hawthorne, Calif. 90250.

Selection Guide for Flowers

Next time you send flowers out of town, you needn't order them blind. A 15-page free selection guide illustrates in full color a variety of bouquets, baskets, wreaths, plants, and arrangements to choose from. Moreover, they can be delivered anywhere in the U.S. or Canada to fit virtually any occasion. Holidays, birthdays, anniversaries, condolences, hospital arrangements, and no-reason-at-all floral gifts are covered. Handy to keep by your telephone. Write: Advertising & Public Relations Div., Florists' Transworld Delivery, P.O. Box 2227, 29200 Northwestern Highway, Southfield, Mich. 48076.

Pep Up Your Power Mower

If you simply pushed your power mower into a corner of the garage last fall after its last mowing session, it's time to be thinking about a spring-cleaning job to ready the machine for the season ahead. Overheating, hard starting, internal engine wear, and other serious problems will result if dirt trapped under, on, and inside your power mower isn't cleaned away. It takes some effort to have a mower that's ready for use any time. A helpful guide, *How to Get Your Power Mower Ready for the Season,* will make that task less troublesome because it covers the nitty-gritty of spring tune-ups. Also tells you how to keep your mower purring. To obtain, send a self-addressed, stamped envelope to: Gumout Div., Pennsylvania Refining Co., Dept. B, 2686 Lisbon Rd., Cleveland, Ohio 44104.

"How to Grow It" Book

Sixteen pages of easy-to-follow instructions tell you how to grow almost anything from gourds to gooseberries to herbs and hedges. Also includes such advice as what grows in moist soil, what in dry, and instructions on flower drying and terrarium gardens. Free from: Gurney's, 4802 Page St., Yankton, S.D. 57078.

Grow Your Own Annuals

Garden annuals are easy to grow, and they do well in all parts of the United States. Whether you want them for yard, window gardens, or as a source of cut flowers, *now* is the time to think of planting seed. A 16-page guide, *Growing Flowering Annuals*, tells how to raise more than 40 different varieties, including the popular marigolds, petunias, ageratum, and zinnias. To obtain, send 45¢ to: Superintendent of Documents, U.S. Government Printing Office, Washington, D.C. 20402, and request bulletin #001-000-03411-1.

Know Your Lawn Seed

What may appear to be the best buy in lawn seed may well result in a poor lawn or an exercise in futility. For instance, *annual* ryegrass dies out after the first year. Even *perennial* ryegrass, which lives about 3 years when planted alone, won't give you a permanent lawn. According to seed experts, the trick in buying lawn seed is to read the label and learn something about the characteristics of different kinds of grasses. A leaflet, *How to Buy Lawn Seed*, can help you be a wise buyer. To obtain, request booklet #001-000-01286-0 and send 45¢ to: Superintendent of Documents, U.S. Government Printing Office, Washington, D.C. 20402.

Bulbs That Bloom in the Spring

Spring-flowering bulbs provide early color in the garden or yard, and are excellent for planting in borders, or scattered in lawns and among shrubs as a ground cover. In most areas, spring-flowering bulbs should be planted in the fall so the roots can develop before the ground freezes. *Spring-Flowering Bulbs* discusses selection of bulbs, planting, care, and forcing. This booklet also includes charts and illustrations and features the well-known spring bloomers—tulip, jonquil, crocus—and some of the uncommon ones—squill, oxalis, winter aconite. To obtain, request publication #001-000-00798-0 and send 45¢ to: Superintendent of Documents, U.S. Government Printing Office, Washington, D.C. 20402.

Know Your Pesticides

Pesticides can be dangerous for man, wildlife, and the ecology. A booklet, *Pesticides and Your Environment,* designed for the home gardener, contains suggestions for controlling pests without pesticides. If pesticides must be used, it suggests those believed to be least damaging to the environment. Free from: National Wildlife Federation, Dept. 001, 1412 16th St., Washington, D.C. 20036.

Indoor Plants

Indoor plants can camouflage ugly radiators; you can make unique plant containers out of old umbrella stands. You can also make your own roof garden, window-box miniature garden, even make your own wall-to-wall indoor garden if you send away for this practical guide, *Selecting and Growing House Plants.* Send 90¢ to: Superintendent of Documents, U.S. Government Printing Office, Washington, D.C. 20402, and request bulletin #001-000-00863-3.

Roses for the Home

Roses can easily be grown in the backyard or garden and are ideal for bouquets, centerpieces, and other floral decorations. You can learn how to cultivate this queen of flowers by sending 45¢ for *Roses for the Home,* #001-000-01511-7, to: Superintendent of Documents, U.S. Government Printing Office, Washington, D.C. 20402.

Trees for Shade and Beauty

Sugar maples don't do well in the fumes and dirt of a city. Norway spruce should never be planted close to a house. Red and silver maples, elms, willows, and poplars are notorious sewer cloggers. . . . If you plan to plant a tree, choose it carefully, and care for it well. For how-to-do-it information, write for *Trees for Shade and Beauty,* bulletin #001-000-01606-7. Send 45¢ to: Superintendent of Documents, U.S. Government Printing Office, Washington, D.C. 20402.

Grow a Garden Indoors

Indoor Gardening With Indoor Sunshine is a brochure for those who talk to their plants and want to grow an indoor garden with indoor sunshine. Advice on quality and quantity of light plants need, as well as humidity, temperature, potting media, fertilizer, watering, ventilation, control of insects, and disease. List of 88 common house plants and degree of hardiness indoors. For free brochure, write to: Duro-Lite Lamps Inc., 17-10 Willow St., Fair Lawn, N.J. 07410.

Wildlife in Your Backyard

Go out in your backyard and look around. Watch the fish weaving among the water lilies, the dragonflies moving in glittering arcs above the little pool. Don't move—the robins are busy feeding their youngsters in that nest above your head; squirrels are edging down the beech trunks behind you and darting into the shrubbery. The wisteria on your stone wall is almost irresistible to the hummingbird that just appeared, and some sparrows are adding their notes to a tangle of birdsong sifting down from the oaks and maples. This isn't your yard, you say? It could be. If you have even a quarter acre of crabgrass right now, you can turn it into a beautiful wildlife habitat. A few square yards—yes, even a window box—can become a wildlife refuge-in-miniature. To transfer this dream into reality, send for the illustrated brochure *Invite Wildlife to Your Backyard.* Free from: National Wildlife Federation, Dept. 001, 1412 16th Street, NW, Washington, D.C. 20036.

The Art of Transplanting

Your evergreen would look better on the other side of the yard. Or your shrub is too crowded. Or that young tree is getting too much shade. Let's move them, you decide. However, if you tell yourself that transplanting a tree or a shrub is nothing more than digging up and planting again, you may be disappointed when your transplant dies. For expert tips on the "what, when, where, and how" of successful transplanting, send for agricultural publication #001-000-03706-4, *Transplanting Ornamental Trees and Shrubs*. It gives step-by-step instructions for digging up and replanting, care of the plant until it becomes established in its new location, and root pruning—the key to moving wild trees and shrubs. To obtain, send 80¢ for mailing and handling to: Superintendent of Documents, U.S. Government Printing Office, Washington, D.C. 20402.

Tips for Turf

The lawn is the most important single feature of the home landscape. You can have a beautiful lawn if you follow the cardinal principles offered in *Suggestions for Fall Lawn Care*. It discusses some of the common causes for poor lawns—mowing too closely, too much traffic, poorly drained soil—and suggests possible cures. Information is given on renovating an old lawn and establishing a new one. Send requests to: Office of Communications, U.S. Dept. of Agriculture, Washington, D.C. 20250.

Color Your Summer

In the heat of the summer the garden's color is usually limited to green, green, and green. If this one-color monotony turns you green, think about adding a few flowering shrubs, vines, and trees for contrast. The great variety of these plants allows home gardeners to choose colors, heights, and shapes for a beautiful garden all summer. A new USDA publication, *Shrubs, Vines and Trees for Summer Color*, can help you to a blooming summer: finding the suitable locations in your garden for the various plants; selecting the plants that bloom harmoniously together or in sequence; choosing the plants that grow well in your area. Now you can plant a nandina, a clematis, or a mimosa. Single copies of publication #001-000-03612-2 are available for 45¢ from: Superintendent of Documents, U.S. Government Printing Office, Washington, D.C. 20402.

For Home Yardeners

A new illustrated 16-page booklet, *Guardin' Your Garden*, tells how to conquer harmful bugs, weeds, and plant diseases via modern garden-spraying techniques. Written by Jerry Baker, noted garden expert and TV personality, the booklet offers spray remedies for 27 common garden ailments such as aphids, crabgrass, and mildew. Baker also discusses the different types of sprayers, the advantage of each, and what features to look for in a compressed air sprayer. As an extra dividend, the author provides a guide to the dos and don'ts of home garden spraying. To obtain, send 35¢ in coin to cover mailing and handling to: Guardin' Your Garden, H.D. Hudson Manufacturing Co., 500 N. Michigan Ave., Chicago, Ill. 60611.

BOOKLETS FOR YARD AND GARDEN

If you want a better lawn, a prettier garden, and a "greener thumb" with flowers, shrubs, and trees, the U.S. Department of Agriculture has the publications to get you started. All are based on USDA research. Pick the ones you think will be most useful. Order from: Superintendent of Documents, U.S. Government Printing Office, Washington, D.C. 20402. Send check or money order—no stamps.

001-000-03740-4	*Better Lawns*	$0.60
001-000-03495-2	*Growing Iris in the Home Garden*	.45
001-000-00864-1	*Pruning Shade Trees and Reparing Their Injuries*	.45
001-000-03419-7	*Growing the Flowering Dogwood*	.45
001-000-02739-5	*Selecting Fertilizers for Lawns and Gardens*	.45
001-000-03411-1	*Growing Flowering Annuals*	.60
001-000-00783-1	*Growing Flowering Perennials*	.90
001-000-03503-7	*Growing Boxwoods*	.45
001-000-03807-9	*Growing Peonies*	.90

Country Xmas Decorations

Fields and woods in autumn and early winter are literally nature's art shop—offering a variety of items in fascinating colors and shapes. Conifer cones, acorns, nuts, dried seed pods, can easily be transformed into wreaths, swags, kissing balls, miniature Christmas trees, corsages, centerpieces—just use your imagination. Add some wire, glue, and patience, and you've created some original holiday hits for your home! Some helpful suggestions for turning nature's materials into your own unique decorations have been prepared in flyer form by USDA horticulturists. Free flyers are available from: Office of Communications, U.S. Dept. of Agriculture, Washington, D.C. 20250.

13

BOUNTY FOR CLUBS, CIVIC GROUPS, CHURCHES

Calling all clubwomen! If you or your husband belong to a social or fraternal society, a church, charity, or civic organization, a PTA or alumni association, this chapter is must reading! Discover how to obtain complete program kits ... outstanding motion-picture documentaries ... fabulous free ideas to raise money for your treasury.

Investing for Women

Have you heard about investment clubs for women? Operated by housewives, these clubs help women learn how to handle their money and at the same time build financially. As all-ladies clubs or with their husbands, members meet regularly to select companies which their studies cause them to believe have bright futures, then pool about $20 each on a monthly basis to invest in the stocks of these companies. For a free pamphlet on how to start your own investment club, write: National Association of Investment Clubs, P.O. Box 220, Royal Oak, Mich. 48068.

Start a Community Garden

Everyone from senior citizens to children are doing it. Grow your own carrots and cucumbers. Plots vary from 10-to-20-feet square for an individual to 200 x 400-feet for a group. Neighborhood gardens and farms provide information and a helping hand in preparing land and obtaining water, seeds, mulch, and compost. See a bright new glow of green amidst brick and concrete. Request a free copy of this brochure, *Community Garden Booklet*, from: Gardens For All, Bay and Harbor Rds., P.O. Box 371, Shelburne, Vt. 05482.

Jump into the Car Pool

Car pools are big news today and will continue to be. Lack of parking facilities and the rising cost of parking has stimulated the car pool revival among commuters. But fuel shortages, gas-eating engines, and skyrocketing prices for gasoline are the greatest motivation. The shared use of automobiles also reduces air pollution and eases traffic congestion. The Car Pool Council has prepared a *Car Pool Starter Kit* with an instruction booklet on how to organize a car pool for various purposes, along with a free bumper sticker. To obtain, send a *long*, stamped, self-addressed envelope to: Reymont Associates, 29-CP Reymont Avenue, Rye, N.Y. 10580.

Publicity for Your Club

A free, expertly written *Publicity Handbook* has been prepared specifically for the thousands of men and women whose volunteer task it is to publicize the activities and projects of their clubs or organizations. It contains step-by-step directions for developing good publicity techniques both in writing and in channeling your club's news most effectively. Tells how to send releases to various news media, how to caption publicity photos, etc. Requests should be sent to: Consumer Services 341, Sperry & Hutchinson Co. 2900 W. Seminary Dr., Dept. 1001, Fort Worth, Tex. 76133. Please send 35¢ to cover cost of handling.

Credit Unions

Credit unions are providing millions of Americans with an incentive to save regularly and borrow wisely from sources of low-cost credit that are not always available otherwise. With interest in consumer matters at an all-time high, thousands are asking for information about organizing credit unions in their place of employment, clubs, churches, unions, offices, fraternal or other associations. If you want to know how credit unions operate, how to start one, and how to join, send for free information. Write to: Public Relations Div., 1001, CUNA, 1617 Sherman Ave., P.O. Box 431, Madison, Wis. 53701.

Better Parking for Your Town

No matter where you live, you are bound to have an important stake in our national preoccupation with "the parking problem." What used to be a major concern of only big metropolitan centers is now spreading to suburban towns and medium and smaller cities. It is time for concerned citizens to take a serious look at mass-transit and parking programs. One way to do it is for civic groups or clubs to undertake a survey of local parking conditions. To help you analyze your community's parking needs and take action to improve the situation, the National Parking Association, a nonprofit organization, has prepared a useful guide. For a free copy, write to: National Parking Association, Dept. M., 1101 17th St., NW, Washington, D.C. 20036.

Fine China and Crystal

Want to show your members something extraordinary and exciting? *Of Earth and Fire* is a unique sound-color motion picture and the winner of numerous coveted film awards. Depicting the handcraftsmanship that goes into the making of world-famous Lenox China and hand-blown Lenox Crystal, this outstanding film is both interesting and educational. To book this free 20-minute film and to obtain additional information on other exciting club ideas, write to: Ellen Lynch, Director, Women's Club Activities, Lenox, Trenton, N.J. 08605.

Kayo Delinquency

For over a century, Boys' Clubs of America have been helping youngsters to grow into good citizens. When a boys' club comes into a community, the youth crime rate plummets. To find out how these clubs work and what a community can do to get one in operation, ask for *Give Them a Place to Go, a Way to Grow.* Write: Boys' Clubs of America, 771 First Ave., New York, N.Y. 10017.

Household Help

Is there a shortage of household workers in your community? If the demand for household workers is to be met, training programs must be available and realistic working standards set. Housewives who would like to implement such a program in their town should send for the booklet *If Only I Could Get Some Household Help!* Write: Women's Bureau, U.S. Dept. of Labor, Washington, D.C. 20210.

Money-Making Ideas for Your Club

Raising money is a major problem in almost every community organization, whether the money is for boosting the club's treasury or for a club-sponsored benefit drive. The 32-page *Ways & Means Handbook* discusses a variety of time-tested fund-raising projects for the ways and means chairwoman. To obtain, send 35¢ to cover mail and handling costs to: Consumer Services, Sperry & Hutchinson Co., 2900 W. Seminary Dr., Fort Worth, Tex. 76133.

Want Cheap or Free Land?

What are the prospects for acquiring free government land? Is there a lot of free land around? How difficult is it to buy public land? How much land is available for sale each year? Contains questions and answers most often asked by individuals who wish to obtain free public land for homesteading or to buy tracts at relatively low cost. For a free booklet, *Can I Really Get Free or Cheap Public Land?* write: Consumer Information Center, Dept. 632G, Pueblo, Colo. 81009.

Stop Drunken Driving

Last year thousands of drunken drivers died at the wheel in accidents they caused, kililng and maiming over 100,000 innocent motorists and their passengers in the process. These deadly statistics can be reversed, however, with your help. For instance, if your state is one of the 26 that still does not have drunk driving laws that meet the standards of the National Highway Traffic Safety Administration, you can help get legislation on the books. If your state has the laws, there are simple things you can do to get them working, fairly and strictly. For a free copy of the booklet *The Drunk Driver May Kill You (What You Can Do to Help Get Him off the Road)*, write to: Safety Director, Allstate Insurance Co., Northbrook, Ill. 60062.

For Your Women's Club

Looking for women's club program materials—free, informative, on a wide variety of subjects? The Woman's Club Service Bureau publishes an annual *Program Aids Bulletin* listing materials free of charge to organized women's clubs. Included are program kits, films, booklets for member distribution. To receive a free bulletin, send the name and address of the person in charge of programs to: Woman's Club Service Bureau, 1301 Ave. of the Americas, New York, N.Y. 10019. Be sure to include the name of your club and the number of members.

Cooking for Small Groups

In preparing food for small groups, such as a club luncheon, a small church or community supper, or a get-together for a big family, there is often the worry of not enough food to go around or piles of food left over. For these occasions, a new government publication can be a big help. *Cooking for Small Groups* suggests 12 lunch and dinner menus and gives more than 35 recipes for main dishes, vegetables, salads, and desserts. Yields of the recipes are 15, 25, or more servings, up to 50, as you need. Tips on how to keep the food safe to eat while it is being prepared and held for serving are included. To obtain, send 45¢ for mailing to: Superintendent of Documents, U.S. Government Printing Office, Washington, D.C. 20402, and request publication #001-000-03210-1.

That Unmentionable Subject

How to Talk With Your Teenager About VD, a film program for adults dealing with communications problems between adults and teenagers in general and on the subject of venereal disease in particular, is available for free loan with supplementary discussion and publicity materials. A program of the Travelers Insurance Companies, it may be obtained from: West Glen Communications, 565 Fifth Ave., New York, N.Y. 10017. Attention: Ms. Claire Walsh.

14

DREAM DIETS FOR WEIGHT-WATCHERS

Compliments of the nation's most expert dietitians, here are medically approved weight-reducing diets to enable you to wage your personal "battle of the bulge." Send away for these pamphlets ... follow their regimens ... and we guarantee you'll soon be saying adieu to avoirdupois. In other words—farewell forever to fatness!

Free Diet Book

If you're a chronic dieter and go on and off the "calorie wagon" whenever you spot a tasty tidbit, you're in a class with millions of others who can't say no to a second helping. An informative 46-page booklet, *Dieting, Yogurt, and Common Sense,* may possibly help save you from spending the rest of your life in the "fatlands." The booklet contains a medically approved 7-day diet, a calorie chart showing which foods are fattening, and a table which lists desirable weights for men and women, depending on height and body frame. To obtain, send 25¢ for mailing and handling to: Common Sense, Dannon Milk Products, 22-11 38th Ave., Long Island City, N.Y. 11101. (This offer limited to readers who reside east of the Mississippi.)

Weight Control Guide

Did you know that overweight is actually a form of malnutrition that results when people eat too much of the *wrong* foods instead of the correct amounts of the *right* ones? To help stimulate an awareness of the importance of good nutrition, the famous Weight Watchers have prepared a helpful brochure, *Nutrition, Weight Control, and You.* In this colorful booklet, Dr. William H. Sebrell, their medical director, provides the answers to many important questions about nutrition and weight control. Free from: Weight Watchers International, 800 Community Dr., Manhasset, N.Y. 11030.

If You Must Skip the Salt

If salt is an objectionable four-letter word in your life-style, because of health reasons, an informative 38-page brochure, *Low-Sodium Diets Can Be Delicious,* offers 100 recipes that are miserly in salt but magnificent in taste. Most importantly, the brochure lists numerous common foods that are high in sodium. For example, did you know that milk and milk products are taboo? Also bran flakes and waffles? And say goodbye to carrots, celery, and beets if you suffer from high blood pressure. You must also avoid all shellfish. Nevertheless, the world can still be your oyster and you can enjoy dishes like sweet and sour spareribs, sauerbraten, and a variety of delicious pies if you use Fleischmann's unsalted margarine and follow their ingenious salt-free recipes. For a free copy, write to: P.O. Box 1-K, Elm City, N.C. 27898.

Achoo? . . . Then Try This Recipe "Cure"

Some of the most common allergies can be triggered by wheat, milk, or eggs, and leaving these no-nos out of a menu can be tricky. However, there is help available. Best Foods has prepared a guide, *Good Recipes to Brighten the Allergy Diet.* It concentrates on the sweet things in life, desserts. But all the cookies, cakes, custards, muffins, fruit dishes, and sauces in this booklet have not been developed so much for what's in them as for what they omit. There are tasty recipes which contain no wheat, no eggs, and no milk, thus making them acceptable to many who must learn to live within the limits of the allergy diet. If this works for you, don't thank us; just say *"Gesundheit!"* to Best Foods' nutritionists. For your free copy, write: Dept. GRA-1001, Box 307, Coventry, Conn. 06238.

Cholesterol-Free Menus

Confused about the cholesterol bugaboo? Should you avoid fats entirely? Or eat nothing but polyunsaturates? A huge, splendidly colored cookbook, *Sensible Eating Can Be Delicious,* features selected recipes for dishes that appeal to the eye and palate and are high in nutrition, yet minimal in calories, saturated fats, and cholesterol. Believe it or not, the table of contents lists such "off-limits" dishes as chicken tetrazzini, orange pecan cake, french-toast sandwiches, and other yum-yums. Each recipe is accompanied by a kitchen-tested calorie count per serving. For your free copy, write to: P.O. Box 1-K, Elm City, N.C. 27898.

Stay Slim With Chicken

Of all the meats to choose from, did you know that chicken, duck, and turkey rank among the *lowest* in calories? A 30-page booklet, *Poultry in Family Meals,* contains the latest information on how to buy, store, and cook all varieties of poultry, and offers numerous recipes for making them enticing to the palate. Along with each recipe is a suggested menu and calorie count. For your free copy, send 45¢ to: Superintendent of Documents, U.S. Government Printing Office, Washington, D.C. 20402, and request booklet #001-000-03338-7.

The Diet Program That May Save Your Life

A Diet for Today, a 31-page booklet produced by the makers of Mazola corn oil, suggests a meal-planning program that may prolong your life. Crash, short-term diets, and chronic calorie counting are not enough. The fact is that most Americans need a new dietary program, one that helps keep calorie and fat intake moderate, replaces some saturated with polyunsaturated fat, and assures enough of all the essential nutrients.

Beginning with brief, clear definitions of such seemingly mysterious terms as "cholesterol" and "atherosclerosis," the booklet moves on to outline nutritionally balanced sample menus and features 30 appetizing recipes for dishes included in these menus. This diet keeps your cholesterol from moderate to low; it lowers total fat consumed; it replaces some saturated fat with polyunsaturated fat; and it keeps calories at a moderate level. In other words, it's just what the doctor ordered. To obtain, write to: A Diet for Today, Dept. DT-1001, Box 307, Coventry, Conn. 06238.

Reduce With Rice

You can shape up your shape with rice. With rice as a basic food in a weight-reducing program, many of the problems that often frustrate overweight people just disappear. A new booklet, *Rice . . . Low-Calorie Menus and Recipes*, provides easy, monotony-proof daily menus which use nutritious rice as a key food. All recipes, developed by dietitians, are calorie-counted and use rice in main dishes, salads, and as a vegetable in eye- and taste-appealing dishes. Among the numerous recipes: rice tuna salad, rice and crab casserole, chicken and rice ring with tomato aspic, rice pancakes with Chinese sauce. To obtain, write to: Rice Council of America, P.O. Box 22802, Houston, Tex. 77027.

Exercises to Control Your Weight

The President's Council on Physical Fitness offers free this excellent brochure on exercise and weight control. What are the weight control fallacies? Should your exercise be moderate or vigorous? This brochure tells you how to keep physically fit and which exercises will make you feel good and look good. For a free copy of *Exercise and Weight Control,* write to: The President's Council on Physical Fitness and Sports, Washington, D.C. 20201.

Yogurt and Common Sense

A pocket calorie counter for a round-the-clock calorie watch will keep you slim and svelte. For calorie counter, assorted recipe leaflets, index cards, and money saving coupons, write: Free Yogurt Information, Home Advisory Service, Dannon Milk Products, 22-11 38th Ave., Long Island City, N.Y. 11101.

15

FREE GOODIES FOR YOUR PET

Sample the spectrum of treats offered in this chapter for the welfare of your pet, and you'll agree with us that the four-footed folk never had it so dandy since Noah built his ark.

How to Raise a Happy Dog

A dog is many images ... a wagging tail ... a playful leap ... a sympathetic bark ... a loyal companion. You love your pet, and you owe him more than a friendly pat on the head. Toward that end, the Ken-L Ration division of the Quaker Oats Company has prepared *How to Care for, Train, and Feed Your Dog*, a 26-page booklet which tells how to raise your new puppy so that he enjoys a great dog's life. Tells how to groom your dog, what you should know about a collar and a leash, how to be a beloved master. Also contains a permanent dog health record, a helpful feeding chart, plus a free bonus 25¢ coupon toward the purchase of any Ken-L ration product. Even Rin-Tin-Tin and Lassie would endorse this book! Free from: Dog Care Booklet, Box 6333, Chicago, Ill. 60677.

Pets From Foreign Lands

Planning to take your pet abroad? Thinking about importing one when you return? An informative guide, *So*

You Want to Import a Pet? will help you understand the regulations covering the importation of pets by residents of the U.S. Covers exotic birds and other forms of wildlife, discusses cages, custom duties on various pets, necessary vaccinations, etc. For a free copy, write: Office of Information and Publications, Bureau of Customs, U.S. Dept. of the Treasury, Washington, D.C. 20226.

Kitten Care Handbook

If you want to ensure that your kitten develops into a healthy, happy cat with a strong, solid body, a lustrous coat, bright eyes, and well-formed teeth, send away for Ralston Purina Company's publication, *Your Kitten's First Year*. This 46-page booklet provides the reader with a short history of the ancestry of cats and a description of the different breeds of cats. It also gives the growth stages of a kitten from birth until it becomes a mature cat, with vital information on feeding, health, first aid, neutering, housebreaking, grooming, protecting your kitten and your possessions, and reproduction. Everything but the cat's pajamas!

As a bonus, there's a valuable journal page for recording vital statistics and medical history. To obtain, send 35¢ in coin to cover handling to: Purina Kitten Care Handbook, P.O. Box 9419, Dept. P, St. Paul, Minn. 55194.

Operation "Pet Move"

When you and your family pull up stakes in your present neighborhood and decide to relocate in a new home, you must realize that your pets require special loving care on moving day. They sense the change and can become unruly. However, their bewilderment and unhappiness can be avoided by advance planning. A booklet, *Moving Family Pets With Loving Care*, offers tips on how to transport dogs, cats, birds, hamsters, etc., depending on how you make your move. All forms of travel are covered— auto, plane, train. Tells what safeguards to take if you are shipping your pet by air, rail, or express. (This booklet was prepared in cooperation with the American Humane Society.) Free from: Atlas Van Lines, Inc., P.O. Box 509, Evansville, Ind. 47703.

Surgical Neutering?

The transition from pethood to parenthood brings about a new way of life for most dogs and cats. In spite of what many people think, motherhood does not "round out" a pet's personality. As a mother, your pet must divide her affection between you and her litter. This may make her irritable and hard to get along with. And parenthood for your pet really means parenthood for you, too. You must share the burden of caring for the newcomers, particularly if they become ill or have other problems mother can't cope with. There is one satisfactory alternative— surgical neutering, so that the pet cannot reproduce. It has many other advantages, too. A sensitively written booklet, *Choose for Your Pet . . . Pethood or Parenthood,* gives the pros and cons. Free from: American Veterinary Medical Assn., 930 N. Meacham Rd., Schaumburg, Ill. 60196.

Vet-Alert

Before adopting a pet . . . before you even bring him into your home . . . take the animal to your veterinarian. He will be checked internally and externally and receive immunizations. Signs of poisoning and other emergencies are also discussed in this handy brochure. For a free copy write to: Vet-Alert, Hill's Pet Products, P.O. Box 148, Topeka, Kans. 66601.

Calling All Pet Owners

The American Humane Association offers a veritable library of helpful pamphlets for pet owners. *Care of Small Animals* discusses hamsters, rabbits, guinea pigs, and mice. *Care of Fish* gives pointers on fish, turtles, lizards, toads, frogs, even alligators. Other *Care of . . .* pamphlets in this series are devoted to birds, dogs, outdoor dogs, cats, horses and ponies, and burros. Single copies of any title are available for 35¢ postage and handling. Send your request to: American Humane Association, P.O. Box 1266, Denver, Colo. 80201.

Free Pets for the Asking

You and your family can acquire a lovable pup—from a police dog to a Peke—for free!

The Society for the Prevention of Cruelty to Animals stands ready to give you a healthy pup, or a fully grown dog, in the pink of physical condition. There's no charge, but you do have to buy a license, which varies in cost state by state.

In New York City, for example, you will find that one of the nation's busiest SPCA's offers free dogs for adoption. Here is the way to go about getting one, and this procedure is fairly typical of the SPCA branches in other cities.

1. You call or write saying you want to adopt a dog.
2. They investigate to see if the dog will have a good home.
3. If they think he will—the dog is yours.

Also, the SPCA gives away free S-shaped rings which you fasten to the dog's collar for the leash. The New York SPCA is at 441 E. 92nd St., New York, N.Y. 10028.

For the nearest dog adoption service, check your telephone directory under SPCA.

And, cat lovers, do not despair. The same associations can provide you with a kitten or a cat which you can adopt.

Watch the Birdie

Bird-watcher buffs have been known to travel miles in all kinds of weather to observe feathered friends. Now a new brochure can help turn the tables: the birds come to the watcher. A colorful publication, *Invite Birds to Your Home*, gives tips to midwestern homeowners on how to attract robins, cardinals, and other birds into their neighborhoods. It suggests how to create a landscape design, and lists food plants you can grow which will attract the birds. To obtain, request publication PA-982 from: Office of Communications, U.S. Dept. of Agriculture, Washington, D.C. 20250.

Dog Care Handbook

What you always wanted to know about making your dog's life happy, but never found out, is all compiled for you in a 108-page manual, *Handbook of Dog Care*. Not only does the publication answer many of the most frequently asked questions on dog care, but the chapters deal with breeds, registration, first day with your dog, housebreaking, feeding, grooming, health, dog owner's responsibilities, correcting bad habits, obedience, tricks, traveling, dog shows, and puppies on the way. The handbook also features a valuable journal page to record your pet's vital information and medical history. To obtain, send 35¢ to cover postage and handling to: Dog Care Handbook Offer, P.O. Box 9419, Dept. P, St. Paul, Minn. 55194.

Nutrition Guide for Pets

Good nutrition is a big plus in pets—just as it is in humans. If you feed your cat and dog a well-balanced pet food, you may never see evidence of poor nutrition. If you don't, this guide tells what signs to watch for. For free copy, write to: Nutrition Guide, Hill's Science Diet, P.O. Box 148, Topeka, Kans. 66601.

Cookbook for Dogs

Finicky pets, as well as those which eat the same canned meat every day without a whimper, will enjoy and benefit from some variety and home cooking. The kind of foods that will keep Fido healthy and how they should be prepared are described in *Cookbook for Dogs,* published by French's, the company that makes People Crackers, dog treats in the shape of firemen, policemen, dogcatchers, burglars, and mailmen. The recipes include such pet-proven dishes as Happy Hound Hash and Ragout á la Rover. The booklet also contains useful tips for dealing with various pup problems such as a visit to the vet, bathing, traveling, grooming, and etiquette. Write to: People Crackers, 1 Mustard St., Rochester, N.Y. 14609.

Cat Care Handbook

If you love your cat, send away for Purina's new *Handbook of Cat Care*, 76 pages of fact-filled, illustrated chapters including "Selection," "Breeds," "Feeding," "Health," "Grooming," "Kittens," and "The Older Cat," plus an all-important journal page on which to record your cat's vital statistics. To obtain, send 35¢ in coin to cover handling to: Purina Cat Care Center, Checkerboard Square, St. Louis, Mo. 63188.

How to Make Safe Toys for Your Cat

Would your kitty like a toy mouse whose ears can't be chewed off? Or perhaps a bouncy brightly colored felt ball or a glittering rattle made from felt, foil, and a small can? *Safe Toys to Make for Your Cat* is a free booklet of colored pictures toys, patterns, and instructions on how to make safe toys for your kitty. He will meow with delight as he lays down to sleep in the little bed you make from this pattern. To obtain free booklet of instructions and patterns, write for: "Safe Toys to Make for Your Cat," Friskies Division, Carnation Co., Box 780, Dept. M, Pico Rivera, Calif. 90665.

For Bird Watchers

You can brighten up your child's nursery with a gay selection of bird pictures, each 5½ x 8½-inches, all of them in natural color. Comes with an educational 4-page leaflet that describes the habitat, nest, and characteristics of each bird. Each picture is accompanied by a separate outline drawing which your child can color. These pictures are sold in sets only. For prices and more information, write for free catalog, *Audubon Aids in Natural Science*. Address queries to: Educational Services, National Audubon Society, 950 Third Ave., New York, N.Y. 10022.

16

IT'S A MAN'S WORLD

As we promised in Chapter 3, herewith bounty for the male animal. (No use spying on these pages, girls, unless you hunt, fix carburetors, or go deep-sea fishing.)

Fishing Movies

A directory of 16-mm films, most of them in sound and color, covers such subjects as fly, bait, spinning, spin-casting, and trolling for everything from bluegills to blue marlin, instruction in proper use of tackle, family fishing. Send a stamped, self-addressed, *long* envelope to: Fisherman's Information Bureau, 20 N. Wacker Dr., Chicago, Ill. 60606. (See Chapter 24 for additional films.)

Calling All Pipe Smokers

Pipe smokers, if you treasure your pipes, a free 28-page booklet on *Pipe Care* is must reading for you. It tells you how to break in your pipe, clean your pipe, rejuvenate a sick pipe. Its section "Hints for Beginners" will tell you the best way to puff on a pipe so that it always stays cool. Available free, with the compliments of the Brown & Williamson Tobacco Corp. Write to: Sir Walter Raleigh, P.O. Box 1739-PB, Louisville, Ky. 40201.

To Retread or Not to Retread

Do you know how a Lincoln-head penny can tell you when your tires have reached the end of the road? *Save Your Tire's Life ... It May Save Yours* shows you a simple way to check your tire's tread depth—a check critical to the tire's life as well as the driver's. It explains the safety and the economic advantages of having your tires re-cycled (retreaded).

A Retread May Be Your Best Tire Buy ... Ask the Experts offers car owners the facts about today's quality retreads. It explains why experts (including jet pilots and race-car drivers) are using retreads. High-lighting the economic, energy, and environmental benefits of retreads, the book-let shows why the recycled tire is one of the few remaining automotive bargains.

Copies of both booklets are available from: Tire Re-tread Information Bureau, Box 28610, Washington, D.C. 20005.

Good News for Traveling Golfers

A free informative directory lists over 725 golf re-sorts, country clubs, and private courses throughout the United States, Canada, Mexico, the Caribbean, and the South Pacific, with information on the facilities, amenities, phone numbers, and location. You will also receive an application for exclusive membership in "The Golf Card," entitling its members to two complimentary rounds of golf (no green fees) on each and every one of the courses listed in *The Golf Traveler.* For a free copy of this 32-page book, *The Golf Traveler,* write: The Golf Card, P.O. Box 8339, Dept. F, 1625 Foothill Dr., Salt Lake City, Utah 84108. For faster service call toll free 1-800-458-4260.

For the Marrying Kind

If you want to get married with all the correct fash-ions, this booklet advises you about announcements and invitations, proper wedding dress, formal or semiformal wedding, responsibilities of the groom, your best man and ushers, the reception and cake cutting. For this 20-page booklet, write: The Marrying Kind, Communications Dept. 1001, After Six Formals, 22nd and Market Street, Philadelphia, Pa. 19103.

Tips for Trips

Do you know how to get the most for your gasoline dollar? A valuable driver's aid, *TraveLogic*, tells how to compute how many miles you get to the gallon and offers tricks for saving fuel while on trips. A 3-page chart reports the amount of mileage you should expect from every type of car. Particularly useful is the section on how to turn a business trip into a vacation. Write: TraveLodge International, P.O. Box 308, El Cajon, Calif. 92022.

Safe Driving in Winter

Be prepared for skidding or getting stuck in a rut. Know special techniques for safe driving on ice and snow. Heed hints and precautions in this brochure obtained free by writing for: "Safe Driving in Winter," U.S. Dept. of Transportation, National Highway Traffic Safety Administration, Washington, D.C. 20590.

Secrets of Bow Fishing and Hunting

There's no more challenging or exciting fresh- or saltwater sport than bow fishing. This is the answer for the bow and arrow hunter who seeks the excitement of the hunt but finds big game out of season. Classified as small game, the most common freshwater species are carp and gar as well as squawfish, dogfish, buffalo, and suckers. For those near salt water, barracuda, stingrays, and sharks provide the supreme thrill. A booklet, *Tips on Successful Bow Fishing*, written by an expert archer, will introduce you to this challenging sport. And while you're at it, request another booklet, *Secrets of Successful Bow Hunting*, which tells how to hunt moving game. One or both free from: Ben Pearson Archery, P.O. Box 270, Tulsa, Okla. 74101.

Driving Tips for All Seasons

From the freeway to the farm, from daylight to dusk, know these road-wise tips. How to drive on spring ice, summer roads after rain, fall roads covered with wet leaves, winter driving through ice and snow. For free booklet, *Practical Driving Tips,* write: American Trucking Associations, Inc., 1616 P St., NW, Washington, D.C. 20036.

Belt and Hose Book

Belts under the hood of your car transmit power to operate your cooling fan and water pump, alternator, power steering, and air conditioner compressor. To avoid expensive and frustrating roadside breakdowns, your belt should be replaced at 20,000-mile intervals. Hoses carry engine coolant to the radiator for temperature reduction, cause faster engine warm-up, maintain constant engine temperature, and control your heating system. Your hose should be replaced every 24 months as part of a winterizing tune-up. A useful booklet, *The Belt and Hose Book,* tells how to determine if these replacements are necessary, and how to do it yourself at minimum expense. Write: Dayco Corp., Marketing Services, 333 W. 1st St., Dayton, Ohio 45402.

Outboards, Ahoy!

Everything the wise waterman wants to know about Evinrude and Johnson outboard motors and OMC Stern Drive engines is included in this valuable 40-page booklet. A mini-encyclopedia of boating basics, it explains in words and pictures the importance of correct transom height, proper motor angle adjustment, boat loading, and how to get the maximum rpm out of your motor. A special 8-page section, *Story of Propellers,* tells how to select the right propeller for any outboard boat. Also included is a vast variety of boating accessories, instruments, etc. Write to: Advertising Dept., OMC Parts & Accessories, Galesburg, Ill. 61401. Or pick up a copy at your nearby Johnson, Evinrude, or OMC Stern Drive dealer.

Fishing in the Thousand Islands

This attractive brochure, with accurate line-drawing illustrations, contains detailed descriptions of the various types of fish to be caught in U.S. and Canadian waters in the Thousand Islands area of the St. Lawrence River, and in Jefferson County, New York. It lists regulations on seasons, daily limits, and license fees. Available free by writing to: Thousand Islands International Council, Dept. TW-89, Alexandria Bay, N.Y. 13607.

Beware the Used-Car Con Artist

The millions of people who buy used cars every year do so for reasons of economy. They either can't afford or are unwilling to pay the price of a new car. Many motorists never buy a new car—they buy a succession of used cars on the premise that after a new car has been used for a year or two the original owner will have taken care of all the little, nagging problems, as well as absorbing some heavy depreciation. But when you buy a used car there are many pitfalls to look out for that can result in monetary loss, frustration, and a real threat to the safety of the car purchaser. A valuable booklet, *Common Sense in Buying a Used Car,* will enable you to fend off the slick salesman's sting. Write: Consumer Information Center, Dept. 505G, Pueblo, Colo. 81009.

Car Care

Wash, polish, pamper your car, and everyone will envy you. All that glitters may not be chrome but aluminum and will retain a shine with care. How to prevent rust and clean your tires. Take a right turn with car polish and yours will be the snazziest on the block. For free booklet, *Car Care,* write to: Consumer Services Center, 1525 Howe St., Racine, Wis. 53403.

Smokeless Tobacco

If the taste of tobacco is what you're after—or if for any reason you can't light up—here's something worth chewing on. This free colorful 24-pager will bring you up-to-snuff on the history, tradition, and modern-day appeal of smokeless tobacco. To join the growing ranks of American men and women who are discovering a matchless form of tobacco that precedes Columbus, send for your free copy of *Smokeless Tobacco.* Write to: Smokeless Tobacco Council, P.O. Box 70, Peekskill, N.Y. 10566.

Is There an Alcoholic in Your Life?

Someone you love has a drinking problem? If he drinks secretly can you recognize early symptoms? What can you do to help? How does AA work? What about recovery—is there hope? For free copy of *Is There an Alcoholic in Your Life?* and an order form listing other available material, write: AA World Services, P.O. Box 459, Grand Central Station, New York, N.Y. 10017.

Free Certificate of Discharge

A veteran's most valuable possession is his certificate of discharge; without it eligibility for various benefits cannot be established. If your original certificate of discharge has been lost or destroyed, you can obtain a new copy free from Uncle Sam. Your request will be promptly filled if you furnish complete identifying information: date of entry into service; date of discharge; unit in which you served; your name, rank, and serial number. Army veterans should write to: Military Personnel Records Center, AGO, 4300 Goodfellow Blvd., St. Louis, Mo. 63120. Navy veterans should write to: Bureau of Naval Personnel, U.S. Dept. of the Navy, Washington, D.C. 20350.

Rod and Reel Home Project

Pretty as a deer rifle and steamlined as a trout rod, the handsomely paneled "sportsman's corner" described in this free plan is designed to live peacefully in a woman's world. Easy to build and functional for use for your sports equipment, it allows you to display your prize gear with pride. To obtain, send requests to: Handyman Plans, Marlite Paneling, P.O. Box 250, Dover, Ohio 44622. Request plan 102.

Guide for Grooms

The *Gingiss Guide for Grooms,* written by the world's foremost male fashion authority, contains a wealth of valuable information on attire, customs, etiquette, and other details of a formal wedding which are the responsibility of the groom. Also answers the questions most often asked

from time of engagement to the honeymoon. Free from:
Gingiss Formalwear, Dept. MW 10, 30 W. Lake St., Chicago, Ill. 60601.

Motor Oil Booklet

Do you own a car? A mower? An outboard motor? A snowmobile? A small plane? All these machines require oil. Your choice of motor oil for any of them can help save you money. Or it can cost you in repairs or lost time. A 34-page booklet, *What You Should Know About Motor Oil*, tells you what a motor oil does, how to read an oil can, how driving affects your engine, etc. It won't make you an expert, but it will enable you to be knowledgeable about the selection of the right motor oils for all the vehicles you own. Write: Quaker State Oil Refining Corp., Box 989, Oil City, Pa. 16301.

Welcome Aboard

Here's a mini-nautical anthology of aquatic facts and figures, history and anecdotes, geared for boating enthusiasts. Also a section on libations for outboard leisure time. Send stamped, self-addressed, long envelope to: Booth's High & Dry Gin, 17th Floor, 1212 Ave. of the Americas, New York, N.Y. 10036.

Help for Hunters

What is the safest color for a hunter to wear? (It's not red.) Why are many hunters susceptible to an optical illusion? What should a hunter do if he discovers he cannot focus properly on the back sight? To learn the answers to these questions and others, study the booklet *Vision and Hunting*. To obtain, send a stamped, self-addressed, *long* envelope to: Communication Division, American Optometric Association, 243 North Lindbergh Blvd., St. Louis, Mo. 63140.

Sports Special

A $500 Bulova sport timer accurate to 1/10 second will be lent free to judges, referees, and other officials to time any amateur sporting event. Official scorers have only to contact their local authorized Bulova Watch dealer for a free loan of this timer. Last year, a total of 12,468 timers were lent by Bulova, through their local jewelers, and were used by officials at 761 sporting events from coast to coast.

Taller Than Our Fathers

Tall or Big Men ... Have you ever wondered why you're taller than others? Why children outgrow their parents? How tall your children will be? What the dress rules are for tall men? Now you can have the answers to all your questions about height, and it won't cost you a cent. This is the most complete study of height available in the U.S. You'll find everything you always wanted to know about height but were too tall to ask, including: "Causes of Tallness," "Living With Height," "Health and the Tall Man," "The Theory of Hybrid Vigor, Height, and Evolution," "Travel and Clothing Tips for the Tall Man." For free copy of booklet *Taller Than Our Fathers,* send name and address, plus your height, weight, and shoe size to: The King Size Co., 109 King Size Bldg., Brockton, Mass. 02402.

Outdoor Safety Tips

Whether hiking 2,404 miles on the Pacific Crest Trail or merely going on a one-day outing to the woods, there's one very important thing to remember: safety in the outdoors. Many of today's Americans who can navigate an urban freeway with ease are at a complete loss when confronted with a forest trail. And their lack of knowledge about the great outdoors can sometimes be a matter of life or death. To help them survive, there's a government booklet, *Outdoor Safety Tips.* Just the right size to fit in your pocket, it tells how to prepare for your trip, what to do if you get lost, how to signal for help, first-aid tips. To obtain, send 45¢ and request booklet #001-000-03427-8 from: Superintendent of Documents, U.S. Government Printing Office, Washington, D.C. 20402.

Free Trails Info for Backpackers

The backpacking outdoor sport is big and getting bigger. If you're a first-timer and would like to join a knowledgeable group for a first outing, ask the International Backpackers' Association (P.O. Box 85, Lincoln Center, Maine 04458), for a free list of their clubs throughout the U.S.A. and elsewhere. A free journal is also available for $1.25 to cover postage and handling.

All Kinds of Consumer Information

Answers about automobiles, gas tips, employment, education, children of all ages, diet and nutrition, housing and health, home maintenance and security. Find your favorite subject by writing for free catalog to: Consumer Information Center, Pueblo, Colo. 81009.

Sunglasses and Your Eyes

Do you know what glare is? How dangerous are ultraviolet rays? What causes snow blindness? Is there a difference between special sunglasses and other outdoor glasses? These answers are in a sunny booklet, *Sunglasses and Your Eyes*. To obtain, write to: Bausch & Lomb Consumer Products Division, Box 3506-36, 1400 Goodman St., Rochester, N.Y. 14602.

Group Camping by Canoe

From picking a route to preparing food this *Group-Camping by Canoe* booklet gives you the tricks and tips for your camping trip. What clothing and personal items to take, camping gear and tents, how to pack food. For free copy, write to: Grumman Boats, Marathon, N.Y. 13803.

Anyone for Golf?

Free membership in the Flying Golfer's Club, sponsored by Eastern Airlines. The bonus for belonging to this unusual club is its free quarterly newsletter, in which you get instructional golf tips from experts, plus information on budget golf vacations. To join the club, write to: Robert J. Bauer, Flying Golfer's Club, Eastern Airlines, Miami International Airport, Fla. 33148.

Problems With Your Golf?

Do you lead with your shoulders or tighten your right hand when you swing? Professional Bob Toski gives detailed instructions on how to cure these faults plus others. To receive free copy of *How to Cure Golf's Six Most Common Faults,* write to: Golf Digest, 495 Westport Ave., Norwalk, Conn. 06856.

"Go West Young Man"

Greeley, Colorado, is named for Horace Greeley, editor of *The New York Tribune,* who urged young men in the post-Civil War era to "Go West." Now the city is urging travelers to "Come West." The city is an hour's drive north of Denver and is a good place to begin a tour of the high plains country of the West. Centennial Village has the second oldest residence in Greeley, a Union Colony house moved in 1976 from its former site on a farm north of town. The house is furnished much as it might have been when built in 1870. Admission to Centennial Village is free, and there is free parking. For a free illustrated folder describing Centennial Village, the Greeley Museum, and the Meeker Memorial home—Nathan Meeker founded Greeley—write or call: Cultural Affairs Dept., Greeley, Colo. 80631; (303) 353–6123.

Repairing Aluminum Boats

You don't have to be an expert to repair dents and punctures in your aluminum boat. It's an easy craft to fix. For free instructions, write to: "Repairing Aluminum Boats," Grumman Boats, Marathon, N.Y. 13803.

How About Swamp Camping With a Canoe?

Most campers avoid swamps and wetlands and miss opportunities to fish and hunt in new areas. Many swamplands offer deer, wild turkeys, hogs, and small game. Angling in a swamp can reward you with bass and bream. Request free brochure from: "Swamp Camping With Canoe," Grumman Boats, Marathon, N.Y. 13803.

'or the Motorcycle Enthusiast

Free annual pamphlet reporting on activities, programs, .ycle safety information, information sheets on helmets 1977), licensing (1978), statistics (1977). Write for this)amphlet of general interest subjects. By mentioning name)f this book in your request you will receive free motorcy- :le helmet decals. Write for pamphlet and decals to: Mo- orcycle Safety Foundation, 6755 Elkridge Landing Road, _inthicum, Md. 21090. Be sure to mention this book for ree decals.

3icycling—Best Way to Go

A well-kept bike is a safe bike. The checklist in this)ooklet tells what you should do to keep your bike in ip-top shape. Be a "biker in action" by joining a bike club. 4sk your Scout leader to take your troop on a bike hike. Join the YMCA for bike activities. How to keep your bike from being stolen. How to register your bike with police. Booklet includes bicycle identification card. For free copy, write to: Bike it Safely, National Safety Council, 444 N. Michigan Ave., Chicago, Ill. 60611.

Do You Have Squeaky Brakes?

EMP Membrane stops disc brake squeak when ap- plied according to directions on packet. Enough to calm the nerves and the noise of one set of disc brakes, EMP is free if you request it on your letterhead and are in the automotive industry. For free packet, write to: EMP Mem- brane, Guardian, 145 No. Beacon St., Brighton, Maine 02135.

Inside Today's Sports

This new monthly sports newsletter gives the inside sports information on a monthly basis, previewing what's coming up and analyzing activities around the sports world. For a sample copy, send 35¢ to: Inside Today's Sports, 17820 East Warren, Detroit, Mich. 48224.

Tennis Anyone?

This game, once considered the genteel sport of the idle rich, has become the active sport of 40 million Americans. How players, from beginners to future pros, should exercise for greater stamina and agility. This pamphlet is full of diagrams in color and shows you the 20 exercises that make a tennis champ. For free pamphlet, *Tone-Up for Tennis,* write to: Armour-Dial Inc., Greyhound Towers, Phoenix, Ariz. 85077.

Boat Buyer's Guide

Free from Chrysler, 24-page *Boat Buyer's Guide* with answers to questions like these: What kind of boat is right for you? How much and what type of power do you need? How do Chrysler boats and power stack up? What about budgeting and financing? This valuable guide is available at your nearest Chrysler Marine dealer, or write: Chrysler Marine Products, P.O. Box 2641, Detroit, Mich. 48231.

Fun Gift

For thrifty tipplers, here's a guide which offers them thirst-aid. Titled *Make Your Own Scotch Whisky,* it provides step-by-step directions for turning barley, malt, and yeast into alcoholic spirits. Also tells you how to convert your entire house into a distillery, so you can do your own blending. As you have probably guessed, this Scotsman's answer to inflation is a tongue-in-cheek do-it-yourself guide. A great fun gift to bring hosts who are stingy with the booze. For your free, unabridged edition, write to: Make Your Own Scotch Whisky, P.O. Box #7, Cooper Sq. Sta., New York, N.Y. 10003.

Rescue Breathing

Save your buddy from drowning, asphyxiation, or electrical shock by the most effective methods of "Rescue Breathing." Be a hero for saving his life. For this free wallet-size card, write to: Public Relations Dept., Aetna Life & Casualty, 151 Farmington Ave., Hartford, Conn. 06156.

17

TREASURE TROVE FOR TRAVELERS

Whether you travel by train or trailer, bus or boat, jet or jalopy, here is a parade of fabulous "freebies" designed to make your next trip a real treat. Included are free maps to make you a king of the road, boons for boaters, air-flight giveaways to float you on Cloud 9!

For the tourist family who would like to see America first, this chapter tells how you can obtain free vacation kits from every state, from border to border. Here you'll find hunting and fishing information for sportsmen, the latest dope on free camping sites, free colorful pictures of scenic attractions. Now, sit back in your easy chair, and let's start on our round-the-world travelogue!

Visit Rhode Island

A 28-page illustrated booklet, *This Is Rhode Island*, reviews the history and traditions of this beautiful New England state. Also describes its vacation attractions, historical shrines, and other highlights. Write to: Department of Economic Development, Tourist Promotion Div., Weybosset Hill, Providence, R.I. 02903.

For a Worry-Free Vacation

Your Vacation Checklist itemizes things to check before you go, ways of minimizing chances of burglary at home while you're away, and games for children while traveling. Also provides space for a mileage and expense record. Write to: Communications and Public Affairs Dept., Kemper Insurance Cos., Long Grove, Ill. 60049.

A "Spirited" Travel Idea

Want a refreshing change of pace during your next vacation or weekend away? Visit an operating winery. There are more than 200 in 22 states. This handy directory, *Wine Country USA*, tells how to find them. For free copy, send 50¢ plus stamped, self-addressed business envelope to: "Wine Country USA," Reymont Associates, 29 Reymont Ave., Rye, N.Y. 10580.

Bike Safety

The cycling mania has infected an astounding 76 million Americans and, in an age when gasoline is becoming increasingly expensive, bikes have become a popular way to travel. Goodyear's new *Bicycle Blue Book* contains 16 pages of text, cartoons, and photographs that provide many riding and maintenance safety tips. Write to: Public Relations Dept., Goodyear Tire & Rubber Co., Akron, Ohio 44316.

Motels Without Frills

If you can't afford a fancy hotel or motel when you hit the road, there are numerous economy inns and modest motels that offer decent, clean accommodations and plain, wholesome food at budget prices. For a list of these bargain stopovers, send a stamped, self-addressed envelope to: American Hotel & Motel Assn., 888 Seventh Ave., New York, N.Y. 10019.

Know Your Fly-Rights

The Civil Aeronautics Board has published a 12-page booklet called *Air Travelers' Fly-Rights*, about the rights of airline passengers. Among the subjects discussed are: pitfalls to beware of when signing up for a charter flight, what to do if "bumped" from a regularly scheduled flight because it has been oversold, and how to receive compensation for lost baggage. Available free from: Publications Service, Civil Aeronautics Board, Washington, D.C. 20428.

Getting a Handle on Luggage

This 24-page consumer guide has tips on selecting luggage, packing, and caring for luggage, and related information—whether traveling by car, plane, train, bus, or cruise ship. For free brochure, send stamped, self-addressed #10 envelope to: Samsonite, Dept. 1001, P.O. Box 38300, Denver, Colo. 80238.

Before You Pack for That Wonderful Trip

How to pack "right" and travel "light" to save money by avoiding overweight luggage costs. A 20-page guide, *Tips on Packing,* offers useful luggage lore. Pack small items—hose, film, cigarettes—into shoes; stuff handbags with handkerchiefs, jewelry, etc. Also suggests basic wardrobe for him and her, plus essential accessories. As a dividend, there's a section on "How Much to Tip" and a valuable checklist of "Important Last-Minute Things to do Before Departure." To obtain free copy, send 50¢ for postage and handling to: Ventura Travelware, Dept. BW, Long Island City, N.Y. 11101.

Discover New York the Y's Way

A free guest pass for a day at a YMCA of Greater New York will be found inside the backcover of this free brochure. *You'll Find What You Want at the Y!* For free brochure, write YMCA of Greater New York, 422 Ninth Ave., New York, N.Y. 10001.

Ship Your Belongings With Feelings of Security

How should you select a mover? Do you know the Dos and Don'ts of moving? How much should it cost you? What should be weighed? How do you check your weight records? These questions and many others are answered

in a free booklet, *Information on Shipping Household Goods.*
For free copy, write to: Interstate Commerce Commission,
Washington, D.C. 20423.

Vacation Checklist

Your car is bulging. Your dog's at the kennel. Your
iron's unplugged. Your plants are watered. Your kids
can't sit still, and the youngest has to use the bathroom
one more time. Before you roll down the road, run down
this vacation checklist to save time, money, and frustration. This free brochure, *Your Vacation Checklist,* includes a
travelogue to record mileage and expenses, games for kids
in the car, and tips to prevent home burglary. For a copy,
send stamped, self-addressed envelope to: Public Request
Desk, Corporate Relations, D-5, Kemper Group, Long
Grove, Ill. 60049.

U.S. Customs International Mail Imports

You have ordered commemorative plates from Europe before and have never paid duty. Why do you have
to pay duty on a plate you recently received? You received
a gift package from your aunt who was traveling abroad.
Are you entitled to receive it without payment of duty?
You wish to return a foreign-made watch to Switzerland
for repair. How can you do this without paying duty when
it comes back? What items are free of duty? What happens
to your parcel if it isn't claimed? How do you locate a
missing or overdue mail parcel? How do you protest the
Customs duty on your mail package? Are you entitled to
any exemptions from duty? These questions and many
more are answered in a new booklet that includes location
and telephone numbers for Customs International Mail
branches. For a free booklet, write to: U.S. Customs International Mail Imports, Dept. of the Treasury, U.S. Customs Service, Washington, D.C. 20229.

The Unique Metals Park

For a memorable trip, visit the Mineral Garden of the
American Society for metals. Located under a huge geo-

desic dome, the exhibit contains a display of ore speci-
mens excavated from mines all over the world. It features
such minerals as galena and sphalerite from southeastern
Australia, rose quartz from Matachewan, Canada, pyrolu-
site, psilomelane, and hausmanite from Brazil, chalcopy-
rite from the Congo, plus scores more of other fascinating
samples. Before you visit, send for the booklet *A Souvenir
From the American Society for Metals,* which lists all the minerals on display. Write: Public Relations Dept., American
Society for Metals, Metals Park, Ohio 44073.

Shelburne Museum

Discover a new look at America by exploring the past
at the Shelburne Museum in Vermont. Thirty-five buildings on 45 landscaped acres. Go aboard the 220-foot-long
sidewheeler S.S. *Ticonderoga.* Coaches, carriages, and sleighs
are in the Horseshoe Barn. Webb Gallery of American Art
exhibits over 300 academic and native works of art. Beach
Lodge displays wild animals trophies and Indian artifacts.
A 525-foot-long scale model (1 inch) of an early circus
parade and circus posters delights all ages. American folk
art of cigar-store figures, weather vanes, trade signs, ships'
figureheads, eagles, tavern signs, are in the Stagecoach
Inn. Variety Unit is filled with glass, china, pewter, scrim-
shaw, dolls, and dolls' houses. There is a Toy Shop, Black-
smith and Wheelwright Shop, a General Store, Apothecary
Shop, Dentist's and Doctor's Offices. Weaving exhibit. Farm
machinery and tools. Live Bee Exhibit. Plan a full day or
more. Picnic area. Cafeteria. Write for free illustrated
brochure to: Shelburne Museum, Box 7, Shelburne, Vt.
05482.

Auto Tape Tours

Design your own itinerary *before* you leave by refer-
ring to simplified map and outlines of Auto Tape Tours
of the following National Parks and locations: Glacier,
Great Smoky Mountains, Rocky Mountain, Gettysburg,
Grand Teton, Banff/Jasper, Yosemite Park, Lancaster/Penn
Dutch Country, and the entire state of California, plus our
newest addition, three tapes on England and two on Ire-

land. Each brochure contains an interesting description of how the taped tour works, tells you where to get them and how much each costs. All tours recommended by leading auto clubs and travel authorities. Working it all out in advance can save you time and money. For free brochures, write: CC Inc. Auto Tape Tours, P.O. Box 385, Scarsdale, N.Y. 10583.

Guidebook for Handicapped Travelers

If you've had trouble planning trips because there's a handicapped person in your family, get this booklet listing almost 90 guidebooks and the addresses for obtaining them. Most are for U.S. cities, a few for foreign travel, one for national parks and monuments. The city guides contain detailed descriptions of public buildings, hotels, recreational facilities, etc., and indicate their accommodations for people with physical defects. For a free copy of *Guidebook for Handicapped Travelers*, write: President's Committee on Employment for the Handicapped, Washington, D.C. 20210.

Coping With Your Car

For motorists on vacation, the National Highway Traffic Safety Administration has a new booklet that tells how to cope with various kinds of auto emergencies, including what to do if you drive your car into a lake. (Escape through the window, since water pressure will hold the doors shut.) It also deals with loss of steering or braking, fires, loss of lights, overheating, hood pop-up, dropped driveshaft, blowouts, and a whole carload of depressing tour-spoilers like that. The booklet, *How to Deal with Motor Vehicle Emergencies*, is free from: Consumer Information Center, Dept. 507G, Pueblo, Colo. 81009.

Free Tickets to TV Shows

Is Hollywood one of your destinations on your next trip to California? Then don't give up this chance to visit a studio and see your favorite show taped. To get tickets, write as far ahead as possible, indicating the shows of your choice, to: ABC Guest Relations, 41–51 Prospect Ave., Hollywood, Calif. 90027; and NBC Guest Relations Ticket Office, 3000 W. Alameda Ave., Burbank, Calif. 91503.

Chicago Visitors' Guide

"Chicago, Chicago . . ." Interested in visiting this famous metropolis? Drop them a note, and they'll be glad to send you their current calendar of events. They offer a complete listing of festivals and special events, museums, sightseeing highlights, zoos, sports, music and entertainment, theater, cinema, tours, shopping, children's activities, restaurants, and accommodations. Free from: Chicago Convention and Tourism Bureau, 332 S. Michigan Ave., Chicago, Ill. 60604.

The Norfolk Tour

If you're a camera hobbyist, bring loads of film with you if you visit Norfolk, the historic Virginia seaport city. Here are just a few of its fabulous attractions: the famed MacArthur Memorial/Museum, the world's largest naval station, elegant historic residences, and the renowned Chrysler Museum of Art. For details of the other landmarks, send for the *Norfolk Tour* pamphlet. Write to: Dept. DCI-Free, Norfolk Visitors Bureau, P.O. Box 238, Norfolk, Va. 23501.

New York on a Shoestring

If you're planning to visit the Big Apple but have a tight budget, you can save mucho dollars by obtaining the fact-jammed, 56-page miser's manual, *The Student Guide to New York*. Includes complete listings of modest and inexpensive hotels and those offering student discounts, economy restaurants, free places to go and things to see, as well as information on the cheapest means of travel between midtown Manhattan and the major airports. For a thrifty Knickerbocker Holiday, request your copy from: CIEE, 777 United Nations Plaza, New York, N.Y. 10017. Please enclose $1.00 to cover mailing and handling for this weighty item.

Air Travel for the Handicapped

Physically handicapped? Don't let your disability spoil your vacation plans. A booklet, *Air Travel for the Handicapped,* published by Trans World Airlines, describes the special services the airline offers if notified in advance. Among the services described are free transportation of passengers' collapsible wheelchairs in the baggage compartment, special meals for those restricted to certain diets, preboarding privileges to avoid the crush, and a waiting wheelchair to take you to and from the plane if required. For a free copy, write: TWA, 605 Third Avenue, New York, N.Y. 10016.

Travel Tips for Your Next Trip

Packing pointers that will keep you well dressed. Minimum basic wardrobe with helpful hints for extras. Precautions for traveling with tots. Basic guidelines for taking Fido along. Chart of slow and peak season round trip fares to Paris. For free copy of *Travel Tips,* write: Air France, P.O. Box 30729, JFK Airport Sta., Jamaica, N.Y. 11430.

Advice for Air Charter Travelers

1. *Consumer's Guide to Air Charters*—explains different types of charter travel, restrictions, and questions you should ask.

2. *Air Travelers' Fly Rights*—a guide to rights on scheduled air services.

3. *Consumer's Guide to International Air Travel*—general information about traveling abroad. These brochures included in series of nine. For free copies write for: Consumers Guide to Travel Information, Consumer Information, U.S. Travel Service, U.S. Dept. of Commerce, Washington, D.C. 20230.

Dayton's "Aviation Afternoon"

Dayton, Ohio, home of the Wright Brothers, offers a self-guiding tour brochure, *An Aviation Afternoon in the*

Birthplace of Aviation. The full-color guide routes the tourist step-by-step in pictures, text, and numbered map through 13 air and space-related adventures. Top attractions include the Aviation Hall of Fame; Hawthorn Hill, home of the Wright Brothers; the Wright-Patterson Air Force Base; and the Air Force Museum. Other highlights: the restored original 1903 Wright plane; the amazing *First Flight Mural,* composed of 163,000 separate mosaic tiles; and the Neil Armstrong Air and Space Museum, whose exhibits give visitors a feeling of participation in space travel. To obtain, write: Aviation Afternoon, Suite 901, 20 E. 46th St., New York, N.Y. 10017.

Importing a Car?

Going abroad and thinking of buying a Rolls-Royce, a Volkswagen, a Toyota, or a Mercedes? Before you spend a dime on a foreign car, it would be wise to know what your customs exemption is, how much duty you will have to pay, how you can apply the exemptions of the members of your family traveling with you, rules about excise tax, and how to obtain temporary license plates before making Customs clearance. All these rules and regulations are spelled out in an informative booklet, *Importing a Car.* It will help you cut away the international red tape. Write: Office of Information and Publications, Bureau of Customs, Washington, D.C. 20226.

Come to a Wonderful Town—Washington, D.C.

What-To-See, Where-To-Stay, and How-To-Save *Weekend Guide.* Have a special time. Have a show time. Have a tasty time. Have a free time. Start planning your vacation to Washington, D.C. This brochure is just a start. It gives you a brief summary of what to do and where to stay, so after you've picked out what sounds like the right hotel, mail the enclosed coupon to the hotel of your choice, and they'll mail you all the details, plans, packages, and ideas you'll need to make your vacation in Washington a perfect one. For free brochure, write: Hotel Association of Washington, D.C., 1219 Connecticut Ave., NW, Suite 300, Dept. J, Washington, D.C. 20036.

Birmingham Travel Kit

Southern hospitality abounds in Birmingham with unique new restaurants and clubs, hotel rooms, conventions, a sports and entertainment complex, and an 1890s Morris Avenue restoration of old-time restaurants and emporiums. If you-all want more information, write: Dept. DCI-Free, Greater Birmingham Convention & Visitors Bureau, Suite 940, First Alabama Bank Building, Birmingham, Ala. 35203.

Chesapeake Bay Circle Tour

A new brochure describing many of the historic landmarks located within the circle around Chesapeake Bay is available free. The historic Chesapeake Bay Circle Tour, a drive-it-yourself excursion, is detailed in a full-color booklet. One of the highlights of the brochure is a large map keyed to places of major interest in American history. The map covers Delaware, the areas of Maryland and Virginia which border the bay, plus the District of Columbia. Recreational activities in the area are described in detail. For a free copy of the *Circle Tour Brochure*, write: Chesapeake Bay Bridge-Tunnel, Dept. FP, Cape Charles, Va. 23310.

Free Ski Map and Handbook

For a weekend or a week where do you ski in Aspen? Map shows skiing areas and handbook tells where to sleep, eat, shop, plus sightseeing spots. For copy of ski map and handbook, write to: Chamber of Commerce, 328 East Hyman Ave., Aspen, Colo. 81611.

Colorado Suntennial Summer

Colorado, the Roof of the Nation, is best known as a skiing paradise, but it is also the home of a sensational warm-weather program, Colorado Suntennial Summer, offered by nine of the state's most famous resort areas. Created in 1976 to coincide with the nation's Bicentennial as well as the state's Centennial, Suntennial Summer is an ongoing program featuring a 6-night package with one rate interchangeable among the nine participants: Aspen, Breckenridge, Crested Butte, Keystone, Snowmass, Steamboat, Tamarron, Vail, and Winter Park. Summer activities in the state include white-water rafting, horseback riding, jeep trips, visits to ghost towns, kayaking, mountain fishing, and high-altitude golf and tennis. The complete Suntennial program is spelled out in an exciting new brochure available free from: Colorado Suntennial Summer, 4382 Grape St., Denver, Colo. 80216.

The Hampton Tour

The Hampton Tour is a self-drive motor tour consisting of ten outstanding features in the oldest English-speaking settlement in America. Attractions include a double-decker bus tour which takes you to the Hampton Institute, Langley Air Force Base, Bluebird Gap Farm, and the Hampton Coliseum; a boat cruise aboard the Kicotan Clipper which carries you through waters once terrorized by pirates, the Norfolk Naval Base, and a stop at historic Fort Wool. For a free brochure, write: Dept. of Conventions and Tourism, 413 W. Mercury Blvd., Hampton, Va. 23666.

For Family Togetherness on the Rhode

For the vacationing family, America's smallest state offers *The Guide to Rhode Island*, which describes points of interest, accommodations, and calendar of events of particular interest, such as Indian museums, animal zoos, miniature railroads, ferry rides, doll collections, and many other unusual small-fry meccas, most of them free. Lists exhibits for the entire family, such as the fabulous toy collection at Chateau SurMer in Newport. Available from: Dept. of Economic Development, Tourist Promotion Div., Weybosset Hill, Providence, R.I. 02903.

Facts About Florida

Want information about moving to Florida, real estate, fishing, vacationing, condominiums, schools, etc.? Florida's largest publisher offers a free catalog of information books which cover everything you want to know about the Sunshine state. Send requests to: Trend Publications, Inc., P.O. Box 2350, Tampa, Fla. 33601.

Fun City Guide

Why do they call New York City "Fun City"? Because it offers more major attractions for the tourist than any other city! A detailed guide, *The Inns and Ins of New York,* describes "the 103½ fun things" you can explore and enjoy in Manhattan. Zoos, shows, sights, unique collections, etc. Available free from: Holiday Inn of New York-Coliseum, 440 W. 57th St., New York, N.Y. 10019.

Wisconsin Annual Events

Gemutlichkeit is the key to Cheese Days in Monroe, Wisconsin. All kinds of Swiss fun and all kinds of Swiss cheese samples. Milwaukee offers the "World's Greatest Musical Festival" and exciting displays of all breeds of horses and all types of industries and businesses. From June to February there are fun festivals, fairs, and how-to workshops. Before planning your vacation in Wisconsin, write for a free brochure to: Wisconsin Annual Events, Division of Tourism, P.O. Box 7606, Madison, Wis. 53707.

Parlez-vous Francais?

You don't have to speak French to discover Paris on foot. Visit the five Paris avenues named for American presidents. Stroll along the most elegant avenue in the world, the Avenue des Champs-Elysées. For art lovers, the Louvre Museum is a must. Your sightseeing tour should include the Eiffel Tower, Notre-Dame Cathedral, Arc de Triomphe. Be sure to explore the flea market, which offers everything second-hand, from precious antiques to outright junk. See how good your bargaining talents are. To obtain a free copy of *Paris á Pied,* write: Air France, P.O. Box 30729, JFK Airport Sta., Jamaica, N.Y. 11430.

Foreign Money Converter

Deak-Perera's pocket-size foreign money converter is full of golden tips for travelers and can be obtained free by sending a stamped, self-addressed envelope to: Deak-Perera, Foreign Money Converter, 630 Fifth Ave., New York, N.Y. 10111.

Free Plant Embargo Booklet

What can you bring home from foreign countries? Americans traveling abroad are confused by the embargo imposed by the Department of Agriculture on plants of other countries. This free booklet details which plants, foods, and animal products tourists are permitted to bring into the U.S., from coffee berries and cars that you can't bring, to seeds and spices that you can bring. To obtain copy, write to: Travelers' Tips, U.S. Dept. of Agriculture, Washington, D.C. 20250.

Big Bundle for Globe-trotters

The International Association for Medical Assistance to Travelers has a fat, free package of useful stuff. In addition to a membership identification card, you get a directory of cooperating physicians (they charge $15 for office visit and $20 for hotel call) in 120 countries. The bundle also includes a "Traveler Clinical Record" to alert foreign physicians to your allergies or history of hypertension, etc., and an immunization chart indicating requirements for every country on the globe. For membership and information package, write: IAMA, 350 Fifth Ave., Suite 5620, New York, N.Y. 10001.

Travel Bonus for Military Retirees

Retired military persons who have their official Armed Services I.D. card are eligible for inexpensive quarters on bases in the U.S. and some 20 foreign countries. There are 8,500 rooms and suites at 245 major military bases available free to traveling officers, enlisted men, and in most cases their families on an overnight or temporary basis. Obtain your official I.D. card from the army and let them be your host.

See the Amazing Sea World

Millions of people, young and old, have visited the fabulous Sea World in Aurora, Ohio. Among its many attractions are 8 live shows, featuring Shamu, the performing killer whale; performing dolphins, sea lions, and otters; and a water ski spectacular. Visit the "kids only" Cap'n Kids World, a nautically themed playland with over 20 activities; the World of the Sea Aquarium; and 18 more fascinating and entertaining exhibits. In just one day at this famous oceanarium and marine life park, you'll see more exotic species of marine life than a sea captain sees in a lifetime of voyages. For an illustrated free color brochure, write: Sea World of Ohio, 1100 Sea World Drive, Aurora, Ohio 44202.

Foreign Language Health Guide

Suppose while traveling you fractured your fibula in France. Needed a prescription filled in Italy. Suffered a severe sunburn in sunny Spain or Mexico. Or were stricken with a toothache in Germany. And couldn't speak a world of the languages of those countries. How would you tell the foreign doctor, dentist, druggist, or other people what's wrong with you or what you want?

Fortunately, help for the ailing American traveling in Europe or Latin America is available in a comprehensive medical phrase minibook, *A Foreign Language Guide to Health Care*. The pocket-sized edition contains 96 pages featuring hundreds of statements and questions covering every medical situation. The phrases are listed in English, followed by their translations and phonetic pronunciations in French, German, Italian, and Spanish. Phrases listed include: "I need a doctor." "I feel dizzy." "It hurts here." "Send for an ambulance." And the all-important, "What are your rates?" Free copies may be obtained from offices of Blue Cross Plans in every city.

The Maryland Story

The Maryland suburbs of Washington, D.C., are just minutes by car from the White House and Washington's other historic attractions and about an hour's drive from either the world port of Baltimore or the capital of Maryland, Annapolis. The state offers a variety of memorable landmarks for the sightseeing tourist: the U.S. Naval Academy; the Peabody Institute; the Babe Ruth Birthplace; the Star-Spangled Banner Flag House Museum; the Calvert Marine Museum; and the University of Maryland's Chesapeake Biological Laboratory. There are scores more places to visit and photograph. You can find them all described in detail, in an illustrated 36-page brochure, *Maryland*. Free from: Div. of Tourist Development, 1746 Forest Dr., Annapolis, Md. 21401.

Southern California

If southern California attracts you, write for free booklets and information to:

All-Year Club Tourist Information Center, 629 S. Hill St., Los Angeles, Calif. 90014.

San Diego Visitors' Bureau, 499 W. Broadway, San Diego, Calif. 92101.

Free Vacation Suggestions

Four Great Lakes states offer free booklets which list fascinating trips you can take in their territories, trips which abound in famous historical and scenic landmarks, and which will enable you to plan a vacation of fun on the water near one of the Great Lakes.

For free information on where to go and what to see and do in these states, write to:

New York State Dept. of Commerce, Room 265, 112 State St., Albany, N.Y. 12207.

Wisconsin Conservation Dept., Room 26. State Office Bldg., Madison, Wis. 53702.

Minnesota Dept. of Business Development, State Capitol, St. Paul, Minn. 55101.

Michigan Tourist Council, 114 S. Walnut St., Lansing, Mich. 48933.

New York Vacationland Guide

Here is a 96-page, full-color guide to the wonderful world of fun in New York State. Tells where to go, how to get there. Gives facts about over 500 resorts and resort areas. Contains information about the many historic landmarks, scenic wonders, children's attractions, museums; hours of opening and admission prices (if any) are included. Also information on boating and camping. Write: New York State Travel Bureau, 99 Washington Ave., Albany, N.Y. 12245.

National Parks

Before you plan to visit one of our majestic National Parks, brief yourself on the highlights you can anticipate on such a tour by writing: National Park Service, U.S. Dept. of the Interior, Washington, D.C. 20240. It will mail you free any of the following booklets describing the wonderlands named:

> *Rocky Mt. National Park, Colorado*
> *Mt. McKinley National Park, Alaska*
> *Mesa Verde National Park, Colorado*
> *Hot Springs National Park, Arkansas*
> *Hawaii National Park, Hawaii*
> *Carlsbad Caverns, New Mexico*
> *Yellowstone National Park*

Wine Tour Guide Free

This tour takes you to more than 225 American Wineries of the East, Midwest, South, Southwest; contains names, addresses, phone numbers, and travel directions plus 22 maps with route numbers to the major wine-growing areas east of the Rocky Mountains. Send 25¢ in coin to: The Association of American Vintners, Box 84, Watkins Glen, N.Y. 14891.

FARAWAY PLACES, FARAWAY LANDS

Holiday Hosteling for Fun

If you enjoy off-the-beaten-track travel, if your budget requires you to watch your dollars, hosteling is for you. The American Youth Hostels, a nonprofit organization, offers information about low-budget travel in 50 countries for students, teachers, church, youth, and service groups, etc. Also tips on year-round travel fun in the U.S.—skiing, hiking, biking, canoeing, sailing, spelunking with hostelers from your own local area, young and old. For details, how to join, and descriptive booklets, send stamped, self-addressed, *long* envelope to: American Youth Hostels, National Campus, Delpane, Va. 22025.

Free Customs Hints

If you're traveling abroad, do you know what you can bring back with you as souvenirs without paying duty? Can you send home articles to yourself, or as gifts to others? Do you have to declare everything you have bought while abroad? You'll find the answers to these and many other questions which perplex overseas travelers in the booklet *Know Before You Go.* For your free copy, write to: Bureau of Customs, U.S. Treasury Dept., Washington, D.C. 20226.

North of the Border

To introduce you to the charm and variety of Canada, the Canadian government suggests planned adventure tours from the border to the Yukon. Here are 100 "spur" trips along and off the scenic 4,787-mile-long highway that links the Atlantic to the Pacific, complete border crossing information, and highway maps showing access routes to Canada. For your free *Trans-Canada Highway Package,* write: Canadian Government Travel Bureau, 1725 K St., NW, Washington, D.C. 20006.

Nassau and Paradise Island

If you're contemplating a trip to Nassau, the sophisticated hub of the Bahamas, and bridge-connected Paradise Island, 800 acres packed with tropical splendor, then the full-color brochure *Love, Peace, Happiness, Adventure, Excitement, Fun, Nassau and Paradise Island* should be right up your alley. Besides a map pinpointing island accommodations, photos of the hotels, and details about them, the brochure offers suggestions on how to fill vacation time from sunup to the wee hours of the morning. A montage of pictures will provide a glimpse of what's in store. Write to: Nassau/Paradise Island Promotion Board, 255 Alhambra Circle, Coral Gables, Fla. 33134.

For the "Fiddler on the Roof" Set

It comes as a surprise to most travelers that France, with approximately 600,000 Jews, has the fourth largest Jewish community in the world. Paris is home to about 375,000 Jews. Did you know that French Jewry includes Marcel Proust, Pierre Mendès-France, Marc Chagall, Marcel Marceau, Simone Signoret, Romain Gary, and thousands of others? A booklet, *A Jewish Guide to Paris,* discusses Jewish museums and other historical and cultural points of interest, scores of synagogues, and a dozen kosher restaurants. Shalom! For your free guide, write to: Air France, Box 30729, New York, N.Y. 10011.

Canal Trips

For the tourist who has been everywhere else, how about a trip through the Panama Canal? If such an excursion intrigues you, send for the free copy of *Locking Through,* a booklet which tells you how to negotiate the Panama locks. Free from: U.S. Army Corps of Engineers, Central Div., Chicago, Ill. 60605.

Canada's Ocean Playground

Nova Scotia is known as "Canada's Ocean Playground"— for good reason, as this large-size, deluxe 40-page brochure will demonstrate. It features breathtaking, beautiful color photographs of quaint fishing villages, deep coves, sandy beaches, winding trails, and the way of life of the Nova Scotians. Write: Dept. DCI-Ocean, Nova Scotia Information Office, 630 Fifth Ave., Suite 3115, New York, N.Y. 10020.

Free "World Books"

Moving to Australia is one of 13 definitive booklets, by country, which offer tips on moving overseas. Each book features a chapter detailing living conditions in the country, how to live successfully there, how to prepare to move overseas, and steps to take upon arrival. The books also offer information on employment, transportation, even language. Another section provides tips on taking your car along, taking care of medical matters, and how to arrange for a foreign bank account. The countries are the United Kingdom, Bahamas, Saudi Arabia, Philippines, Belgium, Portugal, Brazil, Indonesia, West Germany, Singapore, and Japan. To obtain, write: Atlas Van Lines International, 1212 St. George Road, P.O. Box 509, Evansville, Ind. 47703.

18

A CARLOAD OF COOKBOOKS

Prepare yourself for an endless variety of the most mouth-watering journalism: food cues for the busy housewife, business woman, or bachelor—cookbooks that cost you nothing!

The tips which follow can enable you to plan the family's menu for a year without repeating a meal. The free recipes offered are down to earth, easy to follow, and all tested in the kitchens of top food firms.

Not only do these cookbooks cover the art of cookery, they provide tips for specific situations. For example, you can receive free home-on-the-range advice for serving a big buffet spread or dinner party. Special menu books are also available for holidays, festive occasions, barbecues, gourmet meals, fantastic desserts, and odd-type cookery. So now—come and get it!

Budget Recipe Book

Here is a cookbook that protects your pocketbook! Its 36 pages are packed with scores of recipes that are nutritious, tempting, imaginative—and bargain buys. Suggests a varied menu for a whole week. Some of the more interesting dishes include Cheesy Eggs and Pancakes, Hot Turkey Pan-Sans, Festival Polenta, Orange Butterscotch Coffee Cake, Tamale Pie, and Tuna Timbales. There are hints about shopping wisely, storing food safely, how to read labels, and a kitchen safety checklist. For your free copy, write: Balancing Money & Menus, Box 880, Young America, Minn. 55399.

Eater's Digest

Do you have what it takes to be the perfect host or hostess? *The Gold Standard,* a beautifully illustrated 24-page, full-color booklet featuring dozens of recipes by Liquors Galliano, contains exciting cooking ideas for at-home entertaining. Shows you how to prepare an intimate candlelight dinner for 2; a formal dinner for 12; an after-theater supper for 6; a holiday dinner for 12; a cocktail party for 18; a buffet for 16; a ladies' luncheon for 6; a barbecue for 12; and a picnic for 18. The pictures look so good you'll want to eat the pages! This deluxe booklet is available free if you write: Liquors Galliano, P.O. Box 14755, Baltimore, Md. 21205.

Love That Lamb

Succulent meals are quick and thrifty when you make them with economy lamb cuts. A colorful, deluxe booklet offers imaginative recipes which dress up the less familiar cuts of lamb. Sample treats: Scotch Roast (breast stuffed with ground lamb); Curried Hawaiian Lamb Spareribs; Carrot Lamb Loaf; Chili Lamb Riblets—and many more. Included also are interesting accessories to make each dish a hit. Moral: while these dishes cost less, they are no less delicious than more expensive cuts of lamb or beef. To obtain, request a copy of *Economy Lamb Cut Recipes* from: Dept. 1001, Lamb Education Center, 200 Clayton St., Denver, Colo. 80206.

Give a Fig

If you're into natural foods, consider California figs. No longer is the fig tree only thought of as the provider of man's first wearing apparel; instead it is rightly recognized for its ability to produce nature's most nearly perfect gift. A recipe booklet, *California Figs—So-o-o Good,* tells how to prepare such goodies as Fig Graham Squares, Fruit 'n' Cheese Dip, Figs and Creme Caramel, Surprise Muffins, and No Cook Fig Candy. Also available is *California Dried Figs*, special recipes and serving suggestions of Francine York, lovely movie and TV star. Our favorite? It's irresistible Aloha Cookies. For both booklets, send a *long*, stamped, self-addressed envelope to: California Dried Fig Advisory Board, P.O. Box 709, Dept. S-77, Fresno, Calif. 93712.

Nuts to You

If you're nuts about peanuts, then you'll go ape over this collection of new recipes and new twists to old recipes using peanuts and peanut butter. The four-color, 16-page booklet offers 33 hors d'oeuvre, vegetable and salad, main dish, and dessert recipes using America's favorite nut—the peanut. Information about the history and nutrition of peanuts is included, along with tips on cooking with peanuts. Also traces the history of the peanut in America from its introduction to the U.S. by slaves and the invention of peanut butter by a St. Louis physician. Titled *An All-American Nut's Recipe Book*, it includes such historical dishes as Thomas Jefferson's Peanut Soup and Betsy Ross's Boyfriend Cookies. *Note:* This booklet was *not* written by Jimmy Carter. For your free copy, send a *long*, stamped, self-addressed envelope to: All-American Nut Co., 16901 Valley View, Cerritos, Calif. 90701.

Great Dinners, Low Cost

Guess who's coming for dinner? *Six* hearty appetites! And you won't go into shock when you figure the cost of feeding them if you borrow any of the 15 recipes in this gastronomical gold mine, *Great Dinners for Six . . . on a Budget*. Each of these recipes uses an amount of meat or seafood that, before inflation, we might have bought to make a meal for only two or three. These recipes make use of the same amount of meat to create dinners for six. The trick is the judicious use of nutritious, low-calorie fluffy beds of rice to enrich the meal, plus flavorful seasonings. Some sample dishes: Ham Viennese with Rice, Regal Crab Meat Salad, Chicken San Joaquin, Shrimp Cantonese. They're all scrumptious and substantial. No one will starve. Write: Rice Council, P.O. Box 22802, Houston, Tex. 77027.

Easy Does It With Frozen Vegetables

Best cooking methods to make frozen vegetables taste garden fresh. For free copy request from: The California Frozen Vegetable Council, 27 Branan, Suite 501, San Francisco, Calif. 94107.

Throw a Perfect Party

This is an ideal guide for the "in" hostess. How to create a perfect party mix. How to set the party scene. What party games to play, and how to be the perfect host and hostess. Included are rules for the basic home bar and recipes for popular party drinks. Impress your guests with new taste-tempting hors d'oeuvres that are easy to make. Keep partying with one dish suppers that are hearty, satisfying, and easy to serve. Elegant desserts end this evening and make it "a night to remember." For free brochure, write to: V.O. Party Planner Brochure, F.D.R. Station, P.O. Box No. 1622, New York, N.Y. 10022.

Pasta Primer

As you twirl spaghetti strands around your fork or scoop them up in a spoon haven't you wondered about the pasta saga? How to make, shop for, and store this food of goodness? For low budget, free, perfect pasta recipes, write: Pasta Primer, National Macaroni Institute, P.O. Box 336, Palantine, Ill. 60067.

Meatless Main Dishes

Improve family economics with Spinach Casserole, Sweet and Sour Soybeans, or Ratatouille Monterey. Meatless meals will nourish your family and add to your bank account. For 6 free meatless, high protein, very delicious recipes, write: Meals for Millions, P.O. Box 680, Santa Monica, Calif. 90406.

Bonanza Box of Recipes

Best Foods offers a number of recipe folders. Be surprised. Write for a free list of available materials and see what you get. Send postcard to: Best Foods, Dept. LL-1001, Box 307, Coventry, Conn. 06238.

A Taste of Jamaica

Ahh, Jamaica. With Creole Snapper or Coconut Lobster ... you are there. For dessert, Lime Souffle Pie or Banana Delight and your gastronomic juices will be asking for more. For this free 21-page booklet in color write: Jamaica Recipes, Suite 1000, 1320 South Dixie Highway, Coral Gables, Fla. 33146.

Great Dinners for Six—On a Budget

An assortment of 15 main courses that will make you return for seconds and thirds. Write: The Rice Council, P.O. Box 22802, Houston, Tex. 77027.

Cooking With Yogurt

Yummy yogurt recipes made with meat, vegetables, fish, and poultry. Sauces, marinades, soups, and salad dressings made with yogurt. For free copy, send self-addressed envelope to: Colombo Inc., One Danton Drive, Methuen, Mass. 01844.

Cooking With Natural Flavors

The *True to Nature Recipe Books* take the mystery and uncertainty out of making sauces, gravies, and glazes—the extras in cooking that do so much to highlight the natural flavor and eye appeal of food. The techniques are based on cooking with pure natural cornstarch, an ideal thickener for a wide variety of dishes. In addition to sauces and gravies, the booklets include recipes for soups, stews, casseroles, unusual vegetable dishes, puddings, pies, and other desserts. For free copies of both full-color booklets, write to: "True to Nature Recipe Books," Dept. TN-1001, Box 307, Coventry, Conn. 06238.

Be a Six-Minute Chef

If you want to ask your boss to come for dinner, these sensational quick/easy recipes will get you a raise. A collection of easily and quickly prepared recipes developed by award-winning author Carol Cutler for the Closure Manufacturers Association. Each recipe features ingredients packaged in convenient, resealable bottles and jars which can be stored right on the pantry shelf. For a free booklet, *The Six-Minute Chef*, send a stamped, self-addressed business size envelope to: The Six-Minute Chef, Closure Information Bureau, 300 E. 44th St., New York, N.Y. 10017.

Family Guide for Cereals and Pasta

Hearty eating at mealtime with grain products, a good source of food energy at low cost. This free 37-page booklet gives menu suggestions as well as mouth watering recipes from delicious pasta and pilaf to cornbread and cookies. Obtain free copy from: Superintendent of Documents, No. 001-000-03750-1, U.S. Dept. of Agriculture, U.S. Government Printing Office, Washington, D.C. 20402.

Canned Fruit Nutrition Calculator

This tells you which canned fruits are highest in Vitamins. Be nutrition conscious with pears, peaches, applesauce, or apricots. For free calculator write to: California Apricot Advisory Board, 1295 Boulevard Way, Suite H, Walnut Creek, Calif. 94595.

Yogurt and You

Yogurt is not just a funny word. It is nutritious and delicious. Did you know that you can freeze all its 15 flavors? This handy booklet tells you its interesting origins and what to look for besides nutrition. Does it have artificial stuff in it or is it natural? For free brochure, write: "Yogurt and You," Dorothy R. Young, Dannon Co., 22-1138th Ave., L.I. City. N.Y. 11101.

For Bagel Buffs

Devotees of the bagel (the roll with the hole in the middle) will want to explore these unique serving suggestions for Bagel French Toast, Pizza Bagel, Cinnamon Circles. Be first in your circle to introduce these circular conversation pieces! To obtain, send a stamped, self-addressed envelope to: Recipe Ideas, Lender's Bagel Bakery, P.O. Box 7705, Orange, Conn. 06477.

How to Buy Beef

Which is the best buy—blade chuck roast or shoulder arm roast? Blade chuck is more tender, but the shoulder arm has more meat and less waste. The shoulder arm requires only ½ pound per serving against ¾ pound per person for blade chuck. Many more thrifty shoppers like USDA Good grade beef because it usually is more lean. These and other tips on how to buy—and cook—different cuts of beef and how to judge beef quality are explained in *How to Buy Beef Roasts*, bulletin #001-000-03606-8, available for 35¢. Send request to: Superintendent of Documents, U.S. Government Printing Office, Washington, D.C. 20402.

The Smucker Trilogy

Low Sugar Brunch Bunch is a folder that features special surprise menus made with low sugar spreads. The big surprise is that Smucker's Spreads have all the fresh fruit but half the sugars and calories. Pick a brunch to fit your bunch—an eager eight, a picnic six, a family four, a romantic two.

Simply Sensational Syrups lists recipes for glorifying corn fritters, waffles, squash, and puddings with six great fruit syrups: apricot, blackberry, blueberry, boysenberry, red raspberry, and strawberry.

Go Grape is a folder which tells how you can use grape jelly as a natural pepper-upper for breakfast, lunch, or dinner. Really clever recipes for converting any so-so dish into a delight. Obviously concocted by a grape genius. To obtain all three folders free, send a *long*, stamped, self-addressed envelope to: Smucker's Three Folders, J. M. Smucker Co., Strawberry La., Orrville, Ohio 44667.

Meals With a Flair

Recipes for fast and flavorful dishes for indoor and outdoor cooking can be found in French's new booklet

Meals with a Flair. The booklet features 72 kitchen-tested recipes for appetizers, soups, and main courses, including Chinese Beef and Broccoli, Flaming Chicken Supreme, and Country Fried Fish Fillets. Also includes many easy dips, sauces, bastes, and glazes to liven up plain meats and leftovers. Write: R. T. French Co., 9068 Mustard St., Rochester, N.Y. 14609.

Delicious Blueberry Recipes

All new, delicious, easy to prepare blueberry recipes to use with fresh, frozen, or canned blueberries. Also offers valuable tips for efficient freezing and storage. Write to: NABC, P.O. Box 38, Tuckahoe, N.J. 08250, and enclose 25¢ for handling.

Favorite Southern Recipes

You can cook with a new look by trying out these rice recipes from the southern rice-growing area. Dishes such as Arkansas Cumin Rice, Jambalaya, Mississippi Rice Salad, and Texas Hash bring the pungent, spicy taste of the Southland to your table. These and 15 other rice dishes present the South's prize food in its all-American glory. For a copy of *Southern Rice Recipes,* write: Rice Council of America, P.O. Box 22802, Houston, Tex. 77027.

Cooking With Jams, Jellies, and Preserves

The many ways jams, jellies, and preserves can be used to enhance meals are presented in the new booklet *Smucker's Favorite Recipes.* It contains tempting recipes ranging from breakfast suggestions through desserts. Included also are general cooking tips and suggestions for pancake syrups, milk shakes, glazes, and other uses that do not require detailed recipes. Featured in the selections are recipes for such novel treats as Berrypatch Coffee Cake, Baked Grape Burgers, Strawberry Party Cake, Baked Grape Burgers, Strawberry Party Cake, Candied Carrots, Thimble Cookies, Sweet and Pungent Spareribs, Peach Melba Pie, and Roast Cherry Chicken. Now that your taste buds are stimulated, send a stamped, self-addressed, *long* envelope to: Smucker's Favorite Recipes, J. M. Smucker Co., Strawberry La., Orrville, Ohio 44667.

Salmon Treats

Many are the ways with salmon. For example, there's Salmon Supper Loaf, Scalloped Salmon, Quick Deep-Dish Salmon Pie, Salmon Biscuit Roll, Salmon Vegetable Paella, Baked Salmon Pilaf, Salmon Romanoff, and even Salmon Macaroni. For recipes on how to make these original protein dishes—using salmon right out of the can—send for the illustrated booklet *Quick and Easy Ways with Salmon*. Write: New England Fish Co., Pier 89, Seattle, Wash. 98119.

Marvelous New Rice Recipes

Look for what's hiding in your cupboard and you'll probably find rice, which is inspirational, creative, easy to cook, and nutritious. This free brochure offers recipes for any occasion: a company meal, a church bazaar, or a patio party. For brochure, write: Rice Salads, P.O. Box 22802, Houston, Tex. 77027.

Food Label Guide

Do you know how to read food labels so that you can determine which foods supply significant amounts of essential vitamins and minerals? A free booklet, *Food Labels: The Guide to Better Nutrition*, defines such key terms as "enriched," "fortified," and "RDA," which you should look for on the new food labels. Knowing this is critical to planning well-balanced, nutritious meals. To obtain, write to: Vitamin Information Service, Hoffman-La Roche Ins., Nutley, N.Y. 07110.

On Canning

If you're planning to join the 25% of American families already engaged in growing and preserving some of their own food, don't can a single kumquat until you read *Home Food Preservation*, a 100-page booklet that covers the basics of home canning and freezing. Included are instructions for drying fruits and vegetables as well as making jams, jellies, and preserves. For free copy, write: "Home

Food Preservation," Consumer Protection Center, Dept. 664G, Pueblo, Colo. 81009.

Say Cheese

How can you tell what percentage of whipped cream cheese is fat? Which cheeses are lowest in fat? For the true fat facts, send for the booklet *Fat in Cheese*, published by the Switzerland Cheese Association. Send requests to the association at 444 Madison Ave., New York, N.Y. 10022.

Natural Cooking With Spanish Olive Oil

Olive oil is a flavorful oil, which can be used in many ways in the kitchen in its pure, unrefined state. A colorful 24-page booklet, *Cooking the Natural Way with Spanish Olive Oil*, features 48 recipes using ingredients that contain little or no preservatives. There are also some 40 variations and serving suggestions included, all showing how to adapt the Spanish way of cooking to popular American recipes. To obtain, send 35¢ to cover mailing and handling costs to: Spanish Olive Oil Institute, 666 Fifth Ave., New York, N.Y. 10019.

Serve Sausage

Because sausage costs less per serving than fresh meat and is highly nutritious, you'll appreciate the full menu plans and recipes in the *Sausage Sampler*. Tells how to create mouth-watering dishes from bologna, braunschweiger, Dutch loaf, frankfurters, head cheese, liver sausage, cooked salami, and thuringer. Learn how to prepare Frankfurters Alsacienne, Salami con Carne, and Roast Stuffed Bologna. To obtain, send 35¢ in stamps or coins to cover mailing and handling to: Dept. MW, Union Carbide Corp., 6733 W. 64th St., Chicago, Ill. 60638.

Entertaining Italian Style

Serve Sciarda, Italy's most treasured liqueur. Free, intriguing food, drink, and dessert recipes, with color pictures to help guide your preparation. Send stamped, self-addressed, long envelope to: Sciarda, 17th Floor, 1212 Ave. of the Americas, New York, N.Y. 10036.

Escape to the Islands With Tia Maria

A myriad of ways to enjoy this exotic liqueur with its accent of Blue Mountain coffee—an exciting drink and a delicious enhancement for unusual dessert and food dishes. Send stamped, self-addressed, envelope to: Tia Maria, 1212 Avenue of the Americas, New York, N.Y. 10036.

RECIPES AROUND THE WORLD

Oriental Cookery

It's barbecue season and the aroma of pungent flavorings fills the air. Outdoor cooks know that sauces make the difference between a ho-hum barbecue and a great one. La Choy's recipe for Sweet-Sour Chicken Kabobs is sure to establish your reputation as a barbecue chef. La Choy offers free, a full-color booklet which includes a brief history of Oriental cuisines, Oriental cooking techniques, and recipes that when prepared here make you think you're there, China. For free copy, send 50¢ for postage and handling to: La Choy Oriental Recipe Booklet Offer, P.O. Box 211, Dallas, Tex. 75221.

Bacon, Canadian Style

Canadian Bacon Recipes is a refreshing collection of "Baconomy" which offers imaginative dishes like a Canadian Bacon wafflewich, a CB roast, CB canapes, CB waffles with cherry sauce, and CB sandwiches you can make in 2 minutes. Incidentally, did you know that CB has only 9% to 15% fat content, while regular bacon is 60% fat? And if you have to watch your weight, 100 grams of CB contains 260 calories, while regular sliced bacon has 684 calories in the same amount of meat. For your free copy, send a stamped, *long,* self-addressed envelope to: Canadian Bacon Council, Rural Route #3, Barrington, Ill. 60010. (You are invited to send them your original CB recipe; the best entries will win a small gift.)

Favorite Air France Recipes

The French feel about good food as fish feel about water; without it, they simply can't live. Chef Michel Martin presents favorite recipes of Air France passengers that you can try at home, such as Pickled Mushrooms, Stuffed Tomatoes, Beef Stew Provence Style, Chicken Vinegar, Garlic Fried Potatoes, and easy to make desserts. Try these delicious recipes, and *Bon Appétit!* For *French Recipe Booklet*, write: Air France, P.O. Box 30729, JFK Airport, Sta., Jamaica, N.Y. 11430.

New Zealand Lamb

Have you tried the versatile New Zealand lamb? A full-color, 24-page booklet lists simple-to-follow recipes for Lamb Stroganoff, Lamb Chop Linguine Supper, Lamb Tournedos Rossini, Chinese-Style Lamb, Shish Kebabs, Hawaiian Lamb Kebabs, Fondue New Zealand, Lamb Scaloppine, and other dishes that you can sizzle or barbecue. Also tells why frozen lamb is your best meat bargain—a fact worth noting in these inflationary days.To obtain your free copy, write to: New Zealand Meat Producers Board, 800 Third Ave., New York, N.Y. 10022.

A Jewel From Japan-Benihana Recipes

Your favorite hibachi recipes have been adapted for at-home use. Benihana offers recipes of Benihana Chicken, Steak, Shrimp, Magic Mustard Sauce, Magic Ginger Sauce, and others. For free recipes, send #10 self-addressed, stamped envelope to: Ms. Joanie McHale, Benihana-Hardwick, 8685 N.W. 53rd Terrace, Miami, Fla. 33166.

Italian Cuisine

If you like spaghetti with soul, groovy macaroni, and zappy macaroni salad, send for the free recipe booklet *Think Spaghetti*. Tells you the condiments, ingredients, and extras to use, like eggplant, mozzarella, and other *mamma mia* staples. Also suggests noodle dishes that are flipsville for pasta lovers. To obtain, send a *long*, stamped, self-addressed envelope to: National Macaroni Institute, P.O. Box 336, Palatine, Ill. 60067.

Tea for Two or Thirty

Have an English tea party in America? Twinings of London wants to please your palate with sensational tea recipes. A 12-page brochure gives the secrets of heavenly chiffon pie and creamy melon mold made with tea. A sample tea packet is offered with brochure. To obtain this free treat and brochure, write for *Spice n' Easy* to: Dept. M, R. R. Cooper Ltd., 86 Orchard St., Hackensack, N.J. 07601.

There's Nothing Like a Dane!

Hearty open-faced sandwiches and party desserts are described and illustrated in color in *Entertaining in the Danish Manner*. To obtain, send a stamped, self-addressed envelope to: Peter Heering (formerly known as Cherry Heering), 17th Floor, 1212 Ave. of the Americas, New York, N.Y. 10036.

For Lobster Lovers

Colorful 24-page booklet offers dozens of ways to make tempting dishes from the snow-white meat of South African rock lobster tails. Discover easy ways to prepare Lobster Curry, Thermidor, Newburg, and other exotic seafood dishes from Italy, Switzerland, Japan, Spain, China, and France. Send 25¢ in coin to cover cost of postage to: Rock Lobster, Room 3500, 450 Seventh Ave., New York, N.Y. 10001.

Italian Recipes

The famed Bertani Wines of Italy offers a recipe booklet which illustrates favorite examples of Italian cuisine in color. Dishes include stuffed Veal Cutlet and Chicken Breasts Andrès. Naturally, all recipes call for a dash of wine, so there's a helpful wine guide included with the suggested menus. To obtain, write: Bertani Booklet, Carillon Importers, 745 Fifth Ave., New York, N.Y. 10017.

Danish Delights

Venison Medallions. Wild Duck in Cream Sauce. Turkey with Green Grapes. Avocado with Pepper Cream Cheese. Try these specially prepared gourmet recipes on hubby's boss and hubby will win instant promotion to an executive suite! (The trick, of course, is to enhance and mellow these dishes by the addition of Denmark's delicious Peter Heering liqueur.) A handsome, richly illustrated booklet offers these and many other recipes, Chicken Glazed with Aspic, Almond Soufflé, etc. For your free copy, send a stamped, self-addressed, *long* envelope to: Cooking with Peter Heering, 17th Floor, 1212 Ave. of the Americas, New York, N.Y. 10036.

Fancy Coffees Reddi in a Whip

Serve a new yummy drink for that special luncheon or dinner. Mallow-Mint, Melba, or Mocha Deluxe are three of the elegant, easy coffee recipes. Try it—you'll like it. For free brochure, write to: Hunt Wesson Refrigerated Foods, P.O. Box 3800, Fullerton, Calif. 92634.

What's for Dinner?

Delicious Ways to Use Cream of Coconut is a tropical wonderland filled with everything from appetizers like Coco Rumaki and Barbequed Ribs to fabulous beverages like Papaya Thick Shake. Terrific main course recipes include Stuffed Trout, Coco Almondine, and Indian Chicken Curry. Desserts include Creamy Pie and Coconut Crepes. For a free copy, write: Holland House Brands, Dep., C.O., Ridgefield, N.J. 07657.

SEASONS FOR ALL MEALS

Spice Is Nice

Spices and herbs have been prized since the dawn of civilization. Marco Polo and Columbus went looking for them; Shakespeare and Chaucer wrote about them. Today a great variety of spices and herbs are adding tempting aromas and pungent flavors to everyday and exotic dishes.

To add variety and personality to your cooking, here's a list of more than 35 spices and herbs along with the type of foods each can be used with. For a copy of *Seasoning with Spices and Herbs*, send request for publication CA-62-24 to: Information Div., Agricultural Research Service, U.S. Dept. of Agriculture, Hyattsville, Md. 20782.

Abracadabra Flavors

Welcome, range riders, to the *Wish-Bone Dressing Show of Magic and Culinary Wizardry*. Here, right before your eyes, you will discover the real secrets to creating new and memorable recipes. Turn everyday meals into flavorful delights—no slick tricks, nothing up the sleeve—just Italian and Russian dressings from the pantry shelf. With less tender cuts of meat these dressings work marinade wonders. They make these cuts of meat taste better and enhance skillet dinners and barbecue sauces. The result—outstanding dishes like Stuffed Steak Surprise, Ginger Glazed Ham, No-Carve Stuffed Pork Roast, Saucy Spareribs, and Beef Teriyaki. And now, to let the show begin, just say Presto! by ordering a free copy from: Lipton Kitchens, Dept. WB, T.J. Lipton, 800 Sylvan Ave., Englewood Cliffs, N.J. 07632.

The Art of Seasoning

Tabasco, an Indian word meaning "land where the soil is humid," is the trademark for the piquant pepper sauce made by the McIlhenny family of Louisiana. *The Art of Seasoning* describes how the sauce is made, the glories of the Bayou country, and over 60 recipes. For free copy, write: The McIlhenny Co., Avery Island, La. 70513.

All About the Apricot

Did you know that the apricot was discovered in China around 2200 B.C.? That is traveled from the Arab countries to the New World and reached California in the 18th century? In the 20th century we have this free, appetizing *Apricot Booklet* with 66 delicious delectable recipes from Apricot Nut Bread to a Yogurt Apricot drink and a special section on diets: diabetic, low-cholesterol, and high fiber. For free *Apricot Booklet*, write to: The California Advisory Board, 1295 Boulevard Way, Walnut Creek, Calif. 94595.

Avocado Bravo

Tells all about avocados. Recipes for over 100 appetizers, beverages, butters, desserts, fillings, salads, sandwiches, and soups. Includes tips on buying, storing, and ripening. Helpful nutritional advice and instructions on growing an avocado tree from a pit. Send 65¢ to: P.O. Box 19159, Irvine, Calif. 92714.

Food for All Seasons

Let the calendar motivate you. Highlight the seasons with dishes that are complementary. For winter—dishes with fruit syrups that remind you of summer fruits; for spring—Sierra Ranch Ribs that stir vacation memories; for summer—strawberry jam that is so good you will freeze all you can; for fall—your favorite pies, from pecan to pumpkin, to make every day a holiday. For free copy, write to: "Food for All Seasons," Dept. Fas-1001, Box 307, Coventry, Conn. 06238.

Bonanza Box of Herb-Ox Recipes

Thirty-four kitchen-tested recipes on cards for your convenience. Free from: Herb-Ox, P.O. Box 207, Mamaroneck, N.Y. 10513.

DIG THESE DELICIOUS DESSERTS

Ice-cream Recipes

The *Louis Sherry Ice-Cream Almanac* offers ice-cream concoctions that are so yummy you'll want to lick the recipes! Describes how to make a Honey Banana Float, Chocolate Date Pecan Sundae, Rainbow Supreme, Blueberry Ice-Cream Delight, Red Raspberry Cooler, as well as quick 'n' easy ideas for kids. For the "cherry on top," this almanac outlines the history of ice cream since the days of Nero, traces its popularity with George Washington, Thomas Jefferson, Dolley Madison, and other of history's

VIPs. Also discusses the invention of the ice-cream cone and ice cream on a stick. (Sorry, but this offer is limited to readers residing in the areas from Boston to Washington, on the East Coast.) To obtain, send a stamped, self-addressed envelope to: Almanac, Louis Sherry Ice-Cream Co., Dept. MW, 40 Franklin Ave., Brooklyn, N.Y. 11205.

Instant Fruit Dessert Recipes

Apple Fritters, Apricot Cheese Salad, Lemon Broiler Cake, Texas French Toast with Blueberries, Butter Brickle Peach Dessert, Oatmeal Mince Squares, French Apple Coffee Bread, Mock Plum Pudding, Chocolate Cherry Bars, Frozen Fruit Loaf, Raisin Velvet Pie, Strawberry Coconut Custard. This is just a sample of the many instant fruit desserts you can make from Wilderness sweetened, thickened, ready to use, right from the can fruit fillings. Recipes for desserts illustrated in color in and all new, free, 16-page *Wilderness Ways* booklet. To obtain, send 6 × 9-inch self-addressed, stamped envelope to: Wilderness Desserts, Box 6509, Dept. 1001, Duluth, Minn. 55806.

Happy Endings

Contains more than a month of sundaes, cakes, parfaits, pies, and other delights. Super recipes that will get rave reviews from guests and the kids will love. These free happy endings begin with ready-made fresh milk pudding. Write: Swiss Miss, Box 9282-1c, Madison, Wis. 53715, and include 35¢ to cover costs.

THE HOME BARTENDER'S BONANZA

Dine With Wine

Wine makes a meal an occasion, but some people worry about what wine to serve when. The illustrated *Dine With Wine* booklet uncomplicates wine by recommending that you serve whichever one suits your taste. Other hints about the right wine, the right glass, the care and storage of premium qualities are offered along with more than 30 great recipes in the attractive, pocket-sized, 36-page booklet. Free from: Taylor Wine Co., Dept. S, Hammondsport, N.Y. 14840.

Whiskey Recipes and Party Planner

A handy leaflet describing a variety of drinks—cocktails and highballs—that can be made with blended whiskey is yours for the asking. On reverse side is a chart showing the number of drinks needed to entertain different-sized groups at home parties. Write: 90 Proof, Fleischmann Distilling Corp., 625 Madison Ave., New York, N.Y. 10022.

Cordially Yours

Would you like to know how to use cordials, liqueurs, and flavored brandies to add zest to sauces and marinades for meat and poultry, to scent and flavor cakes and cookies? Also how to add sparkle with depth to fruits and soufflés, and to glamorize even simple desserts? An illustrated folder features recipes for cocktail hors d'oeuvres guaranteed to grab the most jaded appetite (all laced with cordial flavors). Also such way-out liqueur concoctions as Mink Fink, Jungle Flower Fantasy, and Chocla Kricket. To obtain, send requests to: Unusual Cordial Recipe Booklet, De Kuyper, P.O. Box 166, Wall Street Sta., New York, N.Y. 10005.

The Tall Drink Mixer That Cooks

As brilliant as a ruby, grenadine is the most versatile of the many flavoring syrups of France. A thirst quencher and drink mixer, it is used in every area of cooking. Perfume a macédoine of fresh fruit with grenadine to give it panache; dazzle your guests with a ham wearing a ruby glaze; mix a little grenadine into plain yogurt; makes milk pretty and delicious for a milk-shy child. Delicious drinks and cocktails plus recipes that will make you a gourmet cook. For free booklet, write: A-W Brands, Inc., P.O. Box 2186 MG, Astoria Sta., New York, N.Y. 11102. (Requests that the booklet be sent to friends or relatives will not be honored.)

Classy Cocktails

Want to impress your guests with the latest "in" drinks? You can offer them original specials like The Gastronaut,

Duke's Special, The Night Parisian, and The Dry Mermaid Martini. For a royal way to treat a friend, serve him a King Peter. Or how about The Hamlet, ideal on a dark, gloomy night when you want to chase away ghosts? To obtain the recipes for these conversational concoctions, send a stamped, self-addressed, *long* envelope to: Drinks with Peter Heering, 17th Floor, 1212 Ave. of the Americas, New York, N.Y. 10036.

Rum Recipes

Have you tried white rum? It smoothes out everything—from screwdriver to Bloody Mary to martini. And all because it's aged in white oak casks for at least 1 full year—by Puerto Rican law. To enjoy this drink, send for a free recipe booklet to: Puerto Rican Rums, Dept. PE-2, 1290 Ave. of the Americas, New York, N.Y. 10019.

Cherry Choices

A new *Something Special* recipe booklet containing more than 20 recipes featuring maraschino cherry products has been published by Liberty Cherry & Fruit Company. The recipes range from Cherry Banana Bread and Cherry Angel Cookies to "Shake-It-to-Me Cherry Nog" and include several dessert ideas. All were developed and tested for yum-yum appeal by Beatrice Foods home economists. Yours for the asking from: Liberty Cherry, Box 808, Covington, Ky. 41015.

How to Choose a Fine Imported Wine

Your special date is coming for dinner. All is ready but the wine. These eleven brochures discuss fine wines to enhance any moment, whether your moment is casual or formal, festive or quiet, or romantically inclined. For free brochures, write: Browne Vinters, Suite 3105, 375 Park Ave., New York, N.Y. 10152.

Ways With Wine

Booklet includes recipes for wine cocktails, mouth-watering stew, and meat sauce for spaghetti that's super.

For free copy, write: "Ways With Wine," P.O. Box 97, Saratoga, Calif. 95070.

The Elegant Adventure—With Wine

How do you savor wine without feeling ridiculous? Why all the fuss about wine glasses? Should you judge a wine by price? What should your basic wine cellar contain? And recipes made with wine that could fetch astronomical prices at an expensive restaurant. For a free booklet, write: Elegant Adventure, Suite 2501, 375 Park Ave., New York, N.Y. 10152.

Want to "Throw an Italian Wine Tasting"?

What a good excuse for a party! A little wine and a little *amóre!* This simple step-by-step guide advises correct setups: how to taste a wine plus wine winning recipes. For free guide, write: "Let's Throw an Italian Wine Tasting," Italian Wine Promotion Center, One World Trade Center, Suite 2057, New York, N.Y. 10048.

Wining and Dining

Food, Fun, and Festivity, a colorful cookbook, provides today's host and hostess with fun ways to use wines and champagnes for festive dining, entertaining, and economical home cookery. Recipe ideas include suggestions for beverages, barbecues, appetizers, soups, salads, fish, poultry, meat, and desserts. An extra feature is a section on the service and storage of wines and champagnes. Write: Mogen David Recipe Book, 75 E. Wacker Dr., Chicago, Ill. 60601.

Drink Book and Cookbook

Do you know how to turn economy cuts of meat into flavorful juicy tenderness with wine? How to make fruit salad shine with wine? How use wine to give hamburgers a driftingly delicious aroma guaranteed to bring out the people next door? You'll learn all these cooking secrets in *Ways with Wine*, a 32-page brochure. Also covers such topics as a home wine cellar, wine tasting, popular drink recipes, champagne parties, and the correct use of glass-ware. Write: Paul Masson Vineyards, P.O. Box 97, Dept. MW, Saratoga, Calif. 95070.

Dine With Dubonnet

A mere tablespoon of wine can liven up salads, sauces, desserts, and beverages. *Les girls* will adore *salade parisienne*, made piquant with Dubonnet blonde. And they will oo-la-la when you serve them cocktail franks simmered in this subtly herbed liquid. Other treats include *Melon Mélange* and an avocado dip guaranteed to make them come back for seconds and thirds. To obtain booklet, write to: Dubonnet, c/o Schenley Importers, 1290 Ave. of the Americas, New York, N.Y. 10019.

Relax at Your Own Party

The Slow Glow is a free, 16-page recipe booklet which offers marvelous menus in color that keep your time and budget in mind. Included are hors d'oeuvres to make on the spot, new ways to serve coffees, and meals to prepare ahead so that you can be the belle of the ball at your own party. For booklet, write: "The Slow Glow," Cointreau, Lawrenceville, N.J. 08648.

Adventures in Good Taste

Want to learn the secrets of good brandy and how it gets its smooth, mellow flavor? Sandeman Brandy tells you this as well as the proper way to serve it from the correct glassware, to flame it, and to add it to your favorite recipes for that gourmet touch. To obtain, send a stamped, self-addressed envelope to: Sandeman Brandy, 17th Floor, 1212 Ave. of the Americas, New York N.Y. 10036.

George Washington Loved It

Quick now, can you name America's oldest native distilled spirit? It's Laird's Apple Jack and it's been around since 1698. Matter of fact, George Washington himself made apple brandy from a recipe he obtained from the

Laird family. You can make your own history with some intriguing ideas from the *Meet Jack Rose* book, including such drinks as an Apple Sunrise or the Big Apple. To obtain, send a stamped, self-addressed envelope to: Apple Jack, 17th Floor, 1212 Ave. of the Americas, New York, N.Y. 10036.

Wine Party Book

Wondering what to serve at that next party? A colorful booklet, the *Almadén Jug Wine Party Book*, suggests recipes for beach parties, soup-and-wine buffets, patio picnics, May winefests, etc. Also offers inventive treats such as Strawberry Wine Pie, Burgundy Burgers, Chicken in Chablis, garnishes for jug wine punches and cocktails, and other unique combinations in the wine world. For a free copy, write to: Almadén Vineyards, Alcoa Bldg., 1 Maritime Plaza, San Francisco, Calif. 94111.

Roman Holiday

What do the following have in common: The Gladiator; Nero's Flame; Forum Flip; Wild Chariot; Julius, Seize Her; Rich Emperor; Via Veneto? No, they're not characters or phrases from a Ben Hur movie; they're all drinks concocted by the ancient Romans from Amaretto, an almond-flavored liqueur made from real Italian almonds, and Sambuca, the licorice-flavored liqueur made from the fruit of the elder bush. Legend has it that these are the potions that turned on Mark Antony and Cleopatra. For drinks and desserts made from these fine patrician liqueurs that will taste like nectar of the gods, write: "The Italian Classics," P.O. Box 14755, Baltimore, Md. 21203.

19

MONEY TALKS!

This chapter is all about money. It may not tell you how to become a millionaire, but it will tell you how to budget money, how to save it, how to spend it wisely, how to invest it, how to borrow it, and even how you may strike it rich. If the advice given here lands you in the lofty income-tax bracket, don't write us for a refund.

Simple Ideas Create Big Profits

For the inventor, amateur or experienced, who can't afford hundreds of dollars for legal fees and is worried about swindlers stealing his idea, here is free protection insurance. Simply send a *long*, self-addressed, stamped envelope to: Flipper, 1046 Dodge Ave., Evanston, Ill. 60202. They will send complete instructions and a form for you to fill out and mail to yourself, with or without witnesses. The method is illustrated for you to duplicate, secretly. This is a legal way of establishing your date of conception and protecting your invention yourself.

How to Strike it Rich

Did you know you can get the government to pay up to half of your cost of exploring for 35 different minerals (e.g., antimony, chromite, gold, iron ore, mercury, mica, silver, and tin)? To get such help you do not have to be an

159

experienced miner, but you do have to show ownership, lease, or other sufficient interest in the property to be explored, and that funds are not available from private sources. If you strike it rich, you will have to repay Uncle Sam with a 5% royalty on your production; if nothing is produced, there is no obligation. For more information, send for the booklet *Exploration Assistance*. Available free from: Office of Minerals Exploration, U.S. Dept. of the Interior, Washington, D.C. 20240.

Avoid Those Budget Blues

Making a partnership of money management—even when there are two incomes—is the best way for a young couple to get off to a good financial start. Since newlyweds are often more romantic than factual about the actual costs of running a household, family economists say they should face money matters frankly. Best idea is to get the problems down on paper, then agree on a realistic spending plan that considers the wishes of both. As circumstances change, adjust the plan. For a copy of *A Guide to Budgeting for the Young Couple*, # 001-000-03702-1, send 90¢ to: Superintendent of Documents, U.S. Government Printing Office, Washington, D.C. 20402.

Must You Sell When the State Wants Your Land?

How was the decision made and how much will you get? What about your house and other buildings on your property? Do you pay capital gains tax on the sale? Can you continue favorable financing? Will your moving costs be paid and what happens if you refuse to sell? Answers to these and other questions are in a booklet entitled *The State Wants My Land . . . Do I Have to Sell?* For a free copy send a stamped, self-addressed long envelope to: Reymont Associates, 29 Reymont Ave., Rye, N.Y. 10580.

Studies in Investing

Is studying techniques a help to developing investment skills? Many individual investors think it's the only way. A new stock study course has been created by the people who for 25 years have helped so many novices and others who have dabbled in the stock market. This home study course can aid your ability to study a stock and make an informed judgment about its potential high and low prices; to compare stocks and select those which appear to offer the greatest opportunity; and to follow stocks you already own and make decisions to sell or buy more. For a free brochure on this stock study course, write: National Association of Investment Clubs, P.O. Box 220, Royal Oak, Mich. 48068.

Planning Your Budget

In these difficult economic times, sound management of your family's money is a good way to make dollars stretch further. A new booklet, *Let's Talk About Money,* helps you plan not only for short-range financial goals but for long-range ones. Step by step you go through a money management process and end up with a program tailored to your specific needs and goals. Handy worksheets in the booklet make the job easier. For your free copy, write to: Institute of Life Insurance, Dept. W, 277 Park Ave., New York, N.Y. 10017.

Make Your Dollars Work

Do you know the four conservative principles for investing? Earn while you learn about money by investing for future security. Write for free brochure, *An Educational and Investment Opportunity for You,* to: National Association of Investment Clubs, P.O. Box 220, Royal Oak, Mich. 48068.

Money Management Booklet Library

Coping with worldwide inflation and raw material shortages is today's greatest challenge. Learn to manage money carefully: to plan, organize, and evaluate personal resources. Be knowledgeable about spending, saving, borrowing, and investing. Free brochure lists booklets you can order for 65¢ each. Write: Money Management Institute of Household Finance Corp., Dept. VTF, 2700 Sanders Rd., Prospect Heights, Ill. 60070.

Should You Buy a Condominium?

Do you want to be your own landlord? When the faucet drips or the paint chips who do you complain to? What does a unit designate? What are advantages and responsibilities of condominium ownership? For free brochure, *Condominium Ownership*, write to: Lawyers Title Insurance Corp., P.O. Box 27567, Richmond, Va. 23261.

Health Insurance

If you're considering purchasing family health insurance, do you know what to look for? *The Health Insurance Answer Book* will acquaint you with many of the terms and provisions you should know in analyzing the major types of health insurance which can protect your family against financial disaster. And it provides checklists of questions for reviewing these provisions as they apply to health insurance for your family. For your free copy, write to: Health Insurance Institute, Dept. X, 277 Park Ave., New York, N.Y. 10017.

A Way to Invest

Interested in investing? An Investment Club can enable men and women of all ages to learn practical finance and build a nest egg in the process. For instance, one group of young men formed a club in 1940. Since then they have invested $108,983, withdrawn $153,643, and still had a liquidating value of $470,675 as of February 28, 1976. Pooling a sum as modest as $20 a month with fellow club members to invest in stocks has provided many investment clubbers' answers to financial goals. For a free pamphlet on organizing your own investment club, write to: National Association of Investment Clubs, P.O. Box 220, Royal Oak, Mich. 48068.

Home Buying Guide

If you plan to buy a house, here's a giant, 160-page book that will answer the thousand and one questions which will arise between the time you first see the real-estate broker and the day you close the deal. Written by an authority, *Home Buying Guide* tells how to figure the real costs, how to deal with a real-estate broker, how to finance a house, how to close the deal, how to determine good construction, etc. There is even a chapter on the differences between cooperative apartments and condominiums. To obtain, send 60¢ to cover mailing and handling to: Lawyers Title Insurance Corp., P.O. Box 27567, Richmond, Va. 23261.

Know the Facts Before Investing

Do you dream of becoming a Ford or a Rockefeller? Do you daydream about earning millions and billions? Before investing your money find out all about Mutual Funds—what they are, the advantages and services offered, can your needs be covered, minimum purchase requirement, retirement advantages. No Load Mutual Fund Association is a nonprofit organization composed of investment companies offering the public an opportunity to invest without any sales commission. For free booklet send $1.00 for postage and handling to: "Your Guide to Mutual Funds Without Sales Charges," No Load Mutual Fund Association Inc., Valley Forge, Pa. 19481.

Can You Manage Your Credit Wisely?

Do you have trouble meeting your installment payments each month? *Managing Your Credit* is a 44-page free booklet that discusses advantages and disadvantages of using credit; tips on establishing and maintaining a regular and revolving charge account; personal installment loans, check-credit plans, cash advances, and second explanatory notes; advice on handling financial difficulties. A chart will aid you in shopping for credit and evaluating its cost. For this easy-to-read, attractively illustrated booklet, send 60¢ with your name and address to: Money Management Institute, Household Finance Corp., 2700 Sanders Rd., Prospect Heights, Ill. 60070.

Ways to Save Time, Achieve More

A 12-page booklet, *How to Add Hours to Your Day*, written by a prominent management consultant, has valuable time-saving tips for executives and business and professional people. Full of practical ideas that can be put to work by anyone to increase efficiency and attain objectives through better time management. For your free copy, write to the publishers: Day-Timers, 3 Willow Rd., Dept. 8037, East Texas, Pa. 18046.

How Much Are Your Bonds Worth?

Do you know how much interest your Government E bonds accumulate each year and how much interest has accumulated if they have matured and you still haven't cashed them in? You will find redemption values in a table published by the Treasury, available from: Superintendent of Documents, U.S. Government Printing Office, Washington, D.C. 20402, for 35¢. And you can get free Treasury circular 653, *Offering of U.S. Saving Bonds, Series A—E*, from your district Federal Reserve Bank, which describes the different bonds and their rates of interest.

Before You Buy Gold Coins

This may be your golden opportunity. Know which coins to buy. How to pay for gold. Is purchase subject to sales tax? Can you buy by mail or phone? Are coins guaranteed? For free brochure of answers, write: "Gold Coins," Deak Perera, Fifth Ave. Inc., Numismatic Division, 630 Fifth Ave., New York, N.Y. 10020.

A Woman's Guide to Insurance

Women are taking an increasingly active role today in planning for their families' future financial needs. A manual, written specifically for women, explains the vital role that insurance plays in this planning and answers questions most frequently asked about insurance. For a free copy of *What Every Woman Should Know About Life Insurance*, write to: Travelers Insurance Co., Women's Information Bureau, 1 Tower Sq., Hartford, Conn. 06115.

Insurance Handbooks

"Plain talk" answers to questions about life and health insurance can be found in a booklet entitled, *50 Questions*

That Help You Get to Know Your Life and Health Insurance Coverage. A sequel to this book, *How to Select the Right Insurance Company,* gives valuable insight into methods you can use to determine the type of insurance company that is best for you. Both booklets are written in an easy-to-read style and are offered free with no obligations. Write: Consumer Services-FT, Bankers Life, Des Moines, Iowa 50307.

Social Security

Wonder how much income you will receive from Social Security when you are eligible for payments? Simply write to: Social Security Administration, Baltimore, Md. 21235. Tell them your age, your social security number, and they'll do the rest.

When Legal Questions Arise

What do you need to know about wills and estate planning? Who will handle your affairs if illness strikes? How should you select an attorney? What are *all* your social security benefits? The answer to these and other questions may be found in *Your Retirement Legal Guide.* For a copy, write: NRTA-AARP, Box 2400, Long Beach, Calif. 90802.

Life Insurance Tips

A 20-page guide, *The Life Insurance Answer Book,* shows you how to use the various kinds of life insurance policies in your financial planning. Discusses such questions as "How can life insurance protect me and my family in case I should be unable to work?" "Do all policies cost the same?" "How do you select an agent?" For a free copy, write to: Institute of Life Insurance, Dept. Y, 277 Park Ave., New York, N.Y. 10017. Also available is a booklet (Dept. Z), *How Much Life Insurance Is Enough?*

Title Insurance Glossary

If you own a home, buy a home, or sell one, whether you're a grantor or a grantee, you'll want to protect your investment with this title insurance glossary. Covers, in alphabetical order, every term from "acceleration clause"

to "wraparound mortgage." Now you'll be able to under-
stand all the esoteric double-talk hidden in the small print.
For a free glossary, write to: Lawyers Title Insurance
Corp., P.O. Box 27567, Richmond, Va. 23261.

Consumer Handbook

Warranties and guarantees are pledges that manufacturers make to customers regarding the materials and
workmanship in their products. If you are considering
buying an appliance, beware of warranties that may be
misleading or deceptive. Do you know how to read a
warranty so that you can tell if the manufacturer is responsible for all defects? Do you know which disclaimers a
company can legitimately establish—damages for which
they are not responsible? To protect yourself, send for the
useful booklet *Warranties & the Consumer*. Free from: Assn.
of Home Appliance Manufacturers, 20 N. Wacker Dr.,
Chicago, Ill. 60606.

20

A TREASURY OF FREE CAREER GUIDES

Attention: Parents, teenagers, college students. Did you know that a wealth of free information on careers in science, aviation, law, public service, teaching, and dozens of other fields is yours for the asking?

For years millions have gone into various fields blindly. As a result, they've fallen into professions for which they were not equipped and have failed sadly. In this age of specialization, such haphazard career choosing can be tragic—and is easily avoidable. For a wise individual can inform himself or his children about a wide variety of interesting and profitable careers—and at no cost.

There is an old saying: "As the twig is bent, so grows the tree." To mix a metaphor, any one of the free career guides in this most important chapter can be the "twig bender" that can enrich your life. All you have to invest is a simple postal card!

Job-Getting Résumé

Applicants—do you freeze when you write your own résumé? This helpful brochure tells you how to put your best foot forward when you're hunting for the right permanent job with a résumé. For a free copy, send stamped, self-addressed envelope to: Western Temporary Services, Inc., Operational Services, P.O. Box 7737, San Francisco, Calif. 94120.

The Right Book for Your Skills

Are you interested in butchering, tool making, or textile printing? Typography, masonry, or metal design? Photography, navigation, or creative canvas work? These are a few of the skills presented in books you can buy from a free catalog. To read about the skill of your choice, write to: Van Nostrand Reinhold, Dept. RB, 135 W. 50th St., New York, N.Y. 10020.

Is Civil Engineering for You?

Did you ever wish you had built the Glen Canyon Dam? Or the Verrazano-Narrows Bridge? Or wished you had designed the huge Vehicle Assembly Building and launch sites at NASA Launch Complex 39 where our manned space vehicles took off for the moon? If you wish you had been involved in any of these or thousands of similar projects, then you would like to be a civil engineer because those are the things civil engineers have done, are doing, will do. For more information about how to qualify for this exciting career, request the illustrated brochure *Is Civil Engineering for You?* from: American Society of Civil Engineers, 345 E. 47th St., New York, N.Y. 10017.

Shorthand Reporting

Shorthand reporting is one of the less-known professions. Yet it is an honored field of work, with ever-growing employment opportunities for young men and women. The work is interesting, and the remuneration compares favorably with that in other fields, ranging from $10,000 to $30,000 a year. The population growth of our country is resulting in a steady increase in the work of our courts and government agencies, and in expanded business and commercial activities. In many areas of the country the demand for the services of the shorthand reporter exceeds the number of entrants in the field. For a copy of *Shorthand Reporting*, write to: Career Desk, National Shorthand Reporters Assn., 2361 S. Jefferson Davis Highway, Arlington, Va. 20202.

Will You Get That Job?

Do you face the personal interview with trembling knees and a queasy stomach? Interviews are double-purposed to find out if you are qualified and if this job is right for you. This free brochure tells all about *The Interview* and can be obtained by sending a stamped, self-addressed envelope to: Western Temporary Services, Operational Services, P.O. Box 7737, San Francisco, Calif. 94120.

Careers in Banking

The United States Treasury's administrator of national banks, the Comptroller of the Currency, is on the lookout for men and women with talent, imagination, initiative, and drive who are interested in devoting themselves to a banking career. National bank examiners evaluate the policies and practices of some 5000 national banks in all the 50 states and the Virgin Islands. The comptroller offers a challenging career with absorbing and varied work assignments and a wide-open future to the young person who qualifies. For information on the specific duties of a bank examiner and qualification requirements, send for the illustrated brochure *World of Banking*. Free to students, teachers, and educational placement advisers from: Comptroller of the Currency, Washington, D.C. 20220.

Careers in Transportation

About to enter college and undecided about your eventual goal? Then investigate the fast-growing, vital field of transportation and its great opportunities. A comprehensive directory lists colleges and universities which offer degrees in traffic management, transportation engineering, highway transportation, transportation economics, marketing, etc. Also available are booklets describing careers in trucking. Free from: American Trucking Assn., 1616 P St., NW, Washington, D.C. 20036.

Careers in Metallury

The field of metallurgy and materials engineering offers exciting opportunities from oceanography to space exploration. Students interested in science and engineering who are about to enter college would do well to study the booklet *A Career in Metallurgy Will Extend Your Reach*, which explores the various roles in this area. Includes information about starting salaries for graduates and a complete list of colleges and institutes which offer programs in this course of study. Available from: Career Guidance Dept., American Society for Metals, Metals Park, Ohio 44073.

Whistle While You Work

Want a job if you are 18 or 88? Required skills are those that meet business needs. After your offspring leave the nest and you retire, the business world needs you for temporary help. Airline stewardess can find temporary work during the several days between flight assignments, as can servicemen's wives whose husbands are ordered to new areas. Combine temporary work with travel. Earn while you learn about new spots and sights. The 100 categories listed range from assignments for the unskilled to the highly trained. For free folder, send stamped, self-addressed envelope to: Western Temporary Services, Operational Services, P.O. Box 7737, San Francisco, Calif. 94120.

Where the Jobs Are for Women

This booklet covers the 15 most promising careers for women, based on information and research from the Business and Women's Professional Foundation. It covers the best career fields for women and gives employment projections for the next 5 years. Obtain free from: Midol Career Booklet, P.O. Box 3899, Rochester, N.Y. 14610.

Overseas Jobs for Women

Women hold 40% of the white-collar jobs performed by Americans overseas. For a teaching position in a military school abroad, write: Schools Recruitment Center, Room 721, Old Post Office Bldg., Washington, D.C. 20315. For information about U.S. Government jobs, order pamphlet #006-000-01033-4 (*Federal Jobs Overseas*) from: Superintendent of Documents, U.S. Government Printing Office, Washington, D.C. 20402, and send $1.00.

A Career in Astronomy

A Career in Astronomy is an informative booklet, which explains the kinds of work astronomers do, lists the opportunities that are available to them, and spells out the specific abilities and academic preparation one needs to work in this field. The pamphlet also lists academic institutions offering undergraduate and graduate instruction in astronomy. An exciting career for those who have stars in their eyes! For your free copy, send 35¢ in coin for postage and handling to: American Astronomical Society, 211 FitzRandolph Rd., Princeton, N.J. 08540.

Need a College Degree?

Need a college degree to get a better job? The College Entrance Examination Board gives placement tests for mature people. You may be able to enter school with course credits. A list of colleges that accept the test and locations where tests are given are available from: CEEB, 1717 Massachusetts Ave., NW, Washington, D.C. 20036.

Be an Appliance Service Technician

Unemployed? Your problems may soon be over if you enter the booming field of the appliance service technician. There is an urgent need for appliance technicians today. Learn how to install, service, and repair dryers, ranges, refrigerators, automatic dishwashers, etc. There are nearly a billion appliances in use today, and not enough skilled labor to maintain them. The U.S. Department of Labor estimates that 220,000 appliance service technicians were employed in 1975 and more are needed every year! For a copy of *Your Career as an Appliance Technician*, write: Assn. of Home Appliance Manufacturers, 20 N. Wacker Dr., Chicago, Ill. 60606.

Beware the Phony Talent Schools

Read *Do You Want to Be an Actor, Announcer, or a Model?* prepared by the American Federation of Television and Radio Artists and the N.Y. State Department of Law. This booklet gives information on how to spot a legitimate agent or worthwhile training school. Legitimate agents, it says, work on a commission and do not ask for a fee in advance. Free from: Dept. of Law, 2 World Trade Center, New York, N.Y. 10047.

Keep an Eye on Optometry

Doctors of optometry are health care professionals who specialize in the examination, diagnosis, and treatment of conditions or impairments of the vision system. Specifically educated, trained, and state-licensed to examine the eyes and related structures to detect the presence of vision problems, eye diseases, and other abnormalities, optometrists are the major providers of vision care in America. If you are interested in the various specialty areas in this profession, such as the prescribing of contact lenses, environmental vision, etc., an interesting booklet, *What Is an Optometrist?* may inspire you to consider a career in this field. For a copy, send a *long,* self-addressed, stamped envelope to: Communications Division, American Optometric Association, 243 North Lindbergh Blvd., St. Louis, Mo. 63141.

The Wild Blue Yonder

Ever toyed with the notion of owning your own plane and earning a good living by operating an air-taxi service, giving joy rides to the public for a price, or cropdusting for farmers by flying over their fields? Before you get your feet off the ground and invest in a plane, learn how you must qualify. A brochure, *A Flying Start,* explains how Private Pilot ratings are obtained. Free from: U.S. Department of Transportation, Publications and Forms Section, TAD-443.1, Washington, D.C. 20590.

Conservation Careers

As our country becomes more and more ecology-conscious the field of conservation will require more specialists to protect our environment: air-pollution control people, landscape architects, foresters who can direct land surveys, road construction, and the planting and harvesting of trees. There are also careers in wildlife conservation and fish conservation. To learn where the jobs are, request the booklet *Conservation Careers* from: National Wildlife Federation, 1412 16th St., NW, Washington, D.C. 20036.

More Than Books

College education is more than books at Antioch College, where students work on regular jobs as well as study. At some 20 centers across the United States and abroad, the Antioch idea combines liberal education with practical experience and specialized studies so that each enlightens and enriches the other. Students work and study in over 30 states and study on the Ohio campus for their B.A. or B.S. degree. Students at the Antioch School of Law, Washington, D.C., begin helping with actual cases along with their classwork. For more information, write to: Antioch Idea, Morgan House, Antioch College, Yellow Springs, Ohio 45387.

The Many Worlds of Civil Engineering

The American Society of Civil Engineering has prepared a helpful series of brochures which zero in on the various, specialized range of subjects in their profession. The series includes: *The Environmental Engineer, The Construction Engineer, The Water Resources Engineer, The Structural Engineer, The Ocean Engineer, The Highway Engineer,* and *The Public Works Engineer.* To obtain any of these illustrated brochures, send your request to: American Society of Civil Engineers, 345 E. 47th St., New York, N.Y. 10017.

A Career in Dentistry

Dentistry offers a wide range of challenging careers. If you are interested in entering this field, now is the time to learn how to qualify. The American Dental Association offers a helpful booklet to guide you: *Dentistry . . . a Changing Profession.* For a free copy, write to: American Dental Assn., 211 E. Chicago Ave., Chicago, Ill. 60611.

"My Son, the Doctor"

If you want to fulfill your parents' ambition that some day you will have an M.D. after your name and have the motivation and qualifications to compete in this limited profession, you'll be interested in the Rochester Plan, a new University of Rochester program designed for students interested in the health professions, including medicine. To obtain, write: Rochester Plan Office, 206A Lattimore Hall, University of Rochester, Rochester, N.Y. 14627. And while you're at it, ask them to send you their service bulletin *So You Want a Career in Medicine?*

Copyright Data

If you are interested in writing, a valuable pamphlet on copyright is available without charge from Daniel S. Mead, prominent literary agent of New York. This information concerning copyrights is presented in condensed form and is of special interest to writers, publishers, lecturers, songwriters, attorneys, playwrights, students, and in fact everyone having an interest in the copyright protection of their creative work. For a free copy, write to: Daniel S. Mead, Box 216, Teaneck, N.J. 07666.

Money-making Opportunities for Writers

The editors of *Writer's Digest,* America's leading writer's magazine, are offering a new 20-page booklet, *Jobs and Opportunities for Writers,* to anyone with a serious interest in writing for profit. This booklet describes the full-time jobs and part-time opportunities available to people with writing skills, and is extremely useful to anyone wanting to make money writing. Get your free copy from: Writer's Digest, Dept. WBJ, 9933 Alliance Rd., Cincinnati, Ohio 45242.

1976 Directory of Accredited Private Home Study Schools

Well over a million Americans from all walks of life are enrolled with the 177 correspondence schools listed in the *1976 Directory of Accredited Private Home Study Schools*. The directory lists hundreds of available courses these students are studying, ranging from art and accounting to welding and writing.

The NHSC Accrediting Commission, which is recognized by the U.S. Office of Education, requires that accredited schools have a competent faculty, offer educationally sound and up-to-date courses, carefully screen students for admission, demonstrate ample student success and satisfaction, and advertise their courses truthfully. Free from: NHSC, 1601 18th St., NW, Washington, D.C. 20009.

THE JOB SEEKER'S JACKPOT

If You Want a Summer Job

Interested in getting a summer job? Even if you're too late to apply for this year, file this away and act promptly early next year. Here are some booklets that might help you:

Summer Employment in Federal Agencies, a 24-page booklet describing federal assistant and trainee jobs open to high-school and college students in various branches of the government, such as the Agricultural Research Service, Department of the Navy, Weather Bureau, Smithsonian Institution, Medicine and Surgery Department, Department of Insurance, etc. Also gives requirements and salaries of the jobs, as well as addresses. For information, write to: U.S. Civil Service Commission, Washington, D.C. 20415.

Employment Opportunities with National Park Concessionaires. Jobs are available for guides, cooks, waitresses, nurses, chauffeurs, and bellboys in the hotels, restaurants, stores, etc., maintained by the concessionaires in the National Parks. This free list, put out by the National Park Service, gives names and addresses of the various concessionaires to whom to write. If you're interested, you'll have to act quickly. Although about 6000 jobs are available, most are taken by the middle of March, and it may take 2 weeks to get the list. Write to: National Park Service, Washington, D.C. 20240.

Giant Career Guide

If you're still unsettled about a career, you'll want a copy of *The New York Times Education Directory*. It includes the advertising of scores of preparatory schools, business schools, professional and vocational schools, and camps. For your free copy, write to: New York Times, School and Camp Dept., Times Sq., New York, N.Y. 10036.

21

YOUR FREE MEDICINE CHEST

Worried about soaring medical costs wreaking havoc with your budget? Take comfort in the knowledge that there is a vast amount of free medical information available.

No, you won't become a doctor by reading this material. And you won't be qualified to treat yourself. However, this literature is a major contribution to everybody's good health. For it alerts you to telltale signs of approaching illness. It teaches you how to recognize the symptoms of major diseases early enough to avoid catastrophic medical expenses, hospitalization, and worse. Thus forewarned, you can go to your doctor for treatment. Not only will you save money, you may save your life. Medical expenses can put you behind the financial eight ball for life. This chapter tells how to avoid or minimize those expenses.

Prevent Tooth Loss

The most common cause of tooth loss among people over 35 is periodontal disease, often known as pyorrhea. It affects half our population by age 50 and most everyone by age 65. This disease is also common among teenagers. Untreated, it always gets worse, requiring long, painful, and expensive surgery. An illustrated booklet, *Research Explores Pyorrhea and Other Gum Diseases*, tell how the problem can be prevented. Write to: Public Health Service, Washington, D.C. 20201, and request publication 1482.

What Do You Know About Contact Lenses?

What are they? Which are dangerous? Are they difficult to use? Are they more effective than regular eyeglasses? What are the advantages and disadvantages? You may obtain this free booklet on *Contact Lenses* by sending a 10-inch long, stamped, self-addressed envelope to: Communications Division, American Optometric Association, 243 North Lindbergh Blvd., St. Louis, Mo. 63141.

Helpful Hints for Handicapped

A publications catalog lists sources for barrier-free environment and careers in rehabilitation. Describes materials that give information concerning physical handicaps and how to adapt. Write for free catalog to: National Easter Seal Society for Crippled Children and Adults, 2023 West Ogden Ave., Chicago, Ill. 60612.

Only for Physical Education Educators

The President's Council on Physical Fitness offers a pamphlet, *The Physically Underdeveloped Child,* free to school physical education teachers, YMCA physical directors, and those who administer standardized physical fitness tests to children. A 3-item screening test identifies young people who fall below minimum standards for strength and endurance. Test instructions for pull-ups, flexed arm hang, and sit-ups. For free pamphlet, write on official stationery to: The President's Council on Physical Fitness and Sports, Washington, D.C. 20201.

Mental Retardation

Valuable information about the care and prevention of mental retardation, including where to go for help, is available in a 26-page illustrated booklet, *Mental Retardation, Its Biological Factors—Hope Through Research*. The brochure explains the various physical and chemical factors that can damage the brain or nervous system and cause mental retardation. The importance of good prenatal care, delivery, and child care is stressed in the prevention of this tragic affliction. Brochure also provides advice about the discovery, care, and training of the mentally retarded child. Send requests on a postal card to: Public Inquiries Branch, Public Health Service, Washington, D.C. 20201.

For Health Teeth

Tooth decay is not inevitable. A government booklet, *Research Explores Dental Decay*, discusses bacteria, nutrition, oral hygiene practices, and other factors that contribute to the development of this disease and tells how you can control them. To obtain, request PHS publication 1483 from: Public Health Service, Washington, D.C. 20201.

For Your Aching Feet

Considering that they must carry us about 65,000 miles in a lifetime, the feet are the most ignored and abused parts of the body. About 7 out of every 10 adults have some form of foot problem. Among the aged, the ratio is 8 out of every 10. Podiatrists are finding that young people, too, are suffering foot ailments in increasing numbers. Expert advice on proper care for foot sufferers is available in a free booklet, *Light on Your Feet*. To obtain it, write: Podiatry Society of New York, Empire State Bldg., New York, N.Y. 10001. Enclose a *long*, stamped, self-addressed envelope.

Children or Adults With Arthritis

Does anyone in your family have arthritis? Don't listen to quacks, faith healers, misery merchants, and other nonexperts. The Arthritis Foundation, the only voluntary health agency fighting a disease that affects 31 million Americans, offers excellent free literature on many aspects of the arthritis problem. Particularly useful are publications on the major forms of the disease: osteoarthritis, rheumatoid arthritis, gout, and juvenile rheumatoid arthritis. The Foundation also provides patients with the names of competent rheumatologists in their areas, as well as locations of local chapters. For free literature, write: Arthritis Foundation, P.O. Box 18888, Lenox Station, Atlanta, Ga. 30326.

A Better Way

Lots of us complain of fatigue, of aches and pains, sore and stiff muscles, the latter especially in the spring when we are prone to exert ourselves after a sedentary winter. Others of us can't relax, or find trouble sleeping, especially those "over 40." An interesting booklet covers research on these subjects, and tells how certain areas of stress can be helped by the Niagara Cyclo-Massage concept. You can have a free copy by writing: Niagara Therapy Corp., Dept. VS, Adamsville, Pa. 16110.

Watch Your Blood Pressure!

You've heard the warnings on TV, you've seen the newspaper ads—high blood pressure is one of the nation's most serious health problems. Yet millions who suffer from this disease are not even aware they have it, because there are no symptoms to discern until it is too late. Most people do not even know what their normal blood pressure should be. They do not even know what the words "systolic" and "diastolic" mean. If you spend hundreds of dollars a year to service your automobile, and hundreds more to take care of your TV set, dishwasher, and other appliances, make the best investment of your life by spending 13¢ for a postal card to get the free booklet *Watch Your Blood Pressure!* Write: Consumer Information Center, Dept. 503F, Pueblo, Colo. 81009.

You and Your Health

You and Your Health is a free booklet featuring 12 articles on major health topics by prominent health experts that originally appeared as a newspaper series. Emergency Reference Chart is included on back cover, and can be kept by telephone. For booklet *You and Your Health*, write to: Council on Family Health, 633 Third Ave., New York, N.Y. 10017.

Don't Be a Vitamin Freak

Once a day, millions of Americans take a multivitamin pill, "just to be sure." Then, when cold season comes around, some stock up on vitamin C. Others whose sex lives seem to be lagging may reach for vitamin E, with the added hope that it will stave off heart disease. And if these vitamins don't prevent that rundown feeling, they'll try all the others. But, according to government experts, consumers should know that the elaborate testimonials and miraculous claims of the vitamin vendors are mere guesswork and often outright fraud. An official report, *Myths of Vitamins*, will prove to you that, while vitamins are essential for good health, excessive amounts are unnecessary and can be harmful. For a free copy, write: Consumer Information Center, Dept. 568G, Pueblo, Colo. 81009.

For Your Aching Back

Backaches are a burgeoning malady afflicting more than 70 million Americans and responsible for an excess of 31 million days of absenteeism from work each year—second only to respiratory infections including the common cold. Many doctors have long recommended a hard bed or bed board for patients with back problems, but until recently there has been no medical standard for firmness. Which is the best bed orthopedic surgeons recommend for victims of this ailment, and why is it best? For the vital facts, send for the booklet, *The Bad Back*, which also suggests tips on basic back care, such as posture, diet, and exercise. Free from: Simmons Co., 1 Park Ave., New York, N.Y. 10016.

Women and Health

This booklet contains 10 articles dealing with health concerns of women. It provides valuable insight into the areas of hypertention, cancer, stress, preventing home accidents, the role of the working mother, medicines and women, pregnancy and childbirth, child abuse, reaching maturity, and nutrition. For a free copy, write for: "Women and Health," Council on Family Health, 633 Third Ave., New York, N.Y. 10017.

Everything You Want to Know About Doctors

If you don't know a pedodontist from a periodontist, better send for a copy of *Facts About Medical and Dental*

Practitioners. Inability to tell one specialist from another can be costly as well as time-consuming when you are looking for medical or dental help. The booklet gives information on types of health professionals, definitions of their titles, their educational requirements, how they specialize, and the scope and limitations of their practice as determined by law. To obtain, send 50¢ to: Superintendent of Documents, U.S. Government Printing Office, Washington, D.C. 20402.

You Too Can Learn Braille Alphabet

What do you do when you see a blind person? What don't you do? What should you do? This brochure gives the correct dos and don'ts. Teach yourself braille alphabet with card of instructions. For free brochure and card write: American Foundation for the Blind, 15 W. 16th St., New York, N.Y. 10011.

Aids for the Blind

Have a friend or relative whose vision is impaired? This 36-page catalog lists items made specifically for nonsighted persons—watches and clocks, household appliances of every kind, tools, games, writing materials, and medical supplies. For free copy, write: "Aids and Appliances," American Foundation for the Blind, 15 W. 16th St., New York, N.Y. 10011.

Home Health Care

As hospitals become increasingly crowded, the supply of nurses and other hospital workers steadily diminishes, and hospital costs continue to spiral at an alarming rate. A brief hospital visit may involve expenses not covered by most health insurance plans, and prolonged hospitalization can spell financial disaster. Fortunately, for many families one alternative already exists—the concept of home health care. If your family physician agrees that home care is feasible for you or your dear one, there are scores of things you should know about treating the patient. Bathroom facilities . . . medications . . . is there a shower or a tub near the patient's bed . . . are there young children in the house? Also, how do you contact the home health care service organization in your community? For all the vital answers, send for the free booklet *What You Should Know About Home Health Care.* For a free copy, write to: Homemakers, Home & Health Care Services, Subsidiary of the Upjohn Co., Kalamazoo, Mich. 49001.

Self-Help Items

A unique mail-order company provides specially designed clothing for handicapped women: "Easy-on, Easy-off" garments, stockings, etc., that are of high quality and fashionable. Also there is a complete line of "Self-Help" items for male and female handicapped individuals. Contains many aids for independent living, such as a one-hand knife, an automatic needle threader, and a no-bend scrubber. For a complete catalog, send 35¢ for mailing and handling to: Fashion-Able, Rocky Hill, N.J. 08553.

Coping With Stress

Stress hits everybody—the aging person, the working man or woman, the student, the adolescent, the child, even the infant. It comes from all directions, and if it isn't avoided or if the individual doesn't cope with it, stress can cause disease and other problems, both physical and psychological. Coping with all forms of this problem is the subject of *Stress,* a 96-page illustrated health education booklet from the Blue Cross system. You can get it free from your local Blue Cross Plan. Also ask for *Food and Fitness,* a practical guide to good nutrition and sensible exercise for all ages.

Free Emergency Chart

You'll be better equipped to handle most medical emergencies with this handy save-a-life chart, "First Aid in the Home," which you can tape to your medicine chest. Gives expert advice on what to do until the doctor comes when a member of the family suffers from inhalation poison, gas, smoke, burns and scalds, shock, broken bones, eye contamination, bleeding, etc. Also tells how to administer artificial respiration via mouth-to-mouth breathing. Free from: Council on Family Health, Dept. MW, 633 Third Ave., New York, N.Y. 10017.

Vitamin E

Are you sneezing or coughing from asthma or hay fever? A pamphlet, *Asthma, Hay Fever and Other Allergies*, may be just what the doctor ordered. Send requests to: Allergy Foundation of America, Dept. GB, 801 Second Ave., New York, N.Y. 10017.

The Truth About Cancer

The American Cancer Society publishes many useful materials on cancer for the public interest. *How to Examine Your Breasts* gives a simple three-step technique for breast self-examination. *Answering Your Questions About Cancer* contains many important facts about early detection of cancer symptoms. *If You Want to Give Up Cigarettes* is an excellent compilation of helpful hints on how to quit smoking. Free copies of any of these publications may be obtained from your local ACS division or unit.

Multiple Sclerosis and Myasthenia Gravis

If you are one of the estimated 500,000 victims of that baffling neurological disease multiple sclerosis, don't spend dollars you can ill afford on hearsay treatment. Contact: National Multiple Sclerosis Society, 205 E. 42d St., New York, N.Y. 10017. They will brief you on the best possible treatment, tell you about the clinic or M.S. chapter nearest your home where you can obtain expert diagnosis and treatment.

Victims of myasthenia gravis can obtain similar free information pertaining to their illness by writing to: Myasthenia Gravis Foundation, New York Academy of Medicine, 2 E. 103d St., New York, N.Y. 10029.

Epilepsy

Of the estimated 2 million Americans afflicted with epilepsy, over 80% can be helped to control their seizures or prevent them entirely. An excellent 27-page pamphlet,

Epilepsy—Hope Through Research, is offered by the Public Health Service in English or Spanish, and explains the causes, symptoms, and control of epilepsy. Tells of current research making possible control of this little-understood disorder and answers questions most often asked by epileptics, their families, and friends. For single free copies of this pamphlet, send requests on a postal card to: Public Inquiries Branch, Public Health Service, Washington, D.C. 20201.

Free Health Aids

The Public Health Service offers two valuable free booklets in their new *Hope Through Research* series: (1) *Headache* is for the sufferer of the occasional headache as well as the victim of migraines. In simple layman's terms, it discusses all types of headaches, their causes and symptoms, tells what you can do about them, when you should go to the doctor. (2) *Hearing Loss* is an illustrated 32-page pamphlet which defines the variety of impairments which afflict millions of Americans. Tells how to guard a child's hearing, the importance of correcting a hearing ailment as early as possible, surgery for otosclerosis, how to choose a hearing aid, ear banks, where to go for help. For single free copies, send requests on a postal card to: Public Inquiries Branch, Public Health Service, Washington, D.C. 20201.

Lung Diseases

The American Lung Association, formerly the National Tuberculosis and Respiratory Disease Association, has been fighting lung diseases for more than 70 years. If anyone in your family suffers from hay fever, asthma, emphysema, chronic bronchitis, tuberculosis, or shortness of breath, free literature is available. Also offered are booklets on cigarette smoking, chronic cough, the common cold, air pollution, influenza, pneumonia, dust diseases, and pleurisy. All or any of these pamphlets are available from: American Lung Assn., 1740 Broadway, New York, N.Y. 10019.

Cleft Palate

If you are one of the more than a quarter million persons in the U.S. afflicted with some form of mouth cleft, a new booklet offers hope. Prepared by the National Institute of Dental Research, it describes cleft lip and cleft palate, and the research on its causes and forms of treatment. To obtain, write to: Public Health Service, Washington, D.C. 20201, and request No. 1487.

Food for Your Heart

Does what you eat have anything to do with heart disease? Are there certain foods that reduce or increase your risks of heart trouble? Your local American Heart Association offers these free booklets:

The Way to a Man's Heart (51-018-A).
Recipes for Fat-Controlled Low-Cholesterol Meals (50-020-B).
A Guide for Weight Reduction (50-034-A).

Choose Your Dentist With Diligence

How do you find a good dental practitioner? Can dental bills be reduced? How effective is fluoridation? Is dental insurance costly and how can you qualify for financial aid for dental care? For answers, write for free pamphlet to: "How to Become a Wise Dental Consumer," 211 East Chicago Ave., Chicago, Ill. 60611.

22

FREE LIFE-SAVERS

During the next 12 months thousands of Americans will commit involuntary suicide. Their methods of self-destruction will include every variety of extinction known to the morgue-keeper's blotter. Thousands will die in automobile accidents. Other thousands will die in home accidents, in fires, and in storms. Hundreds more will succumb via drowning or accidental electrocution.

The common denominator in this annual grim toll of untimely deaths is a low safety IQ. You may think you know how to stay alive, but don't bet on it. The free "life-savers" we have rounded up from the safety experts—to pass on to you—may possibly save your life, or the life of a loved one.

Tire Manual

You can avoid being a highway statistic if you let the safety experts tell you how to break in new tires, what pressure and load limits are safe, how to inspect for tire wear and damage, what to watch for when repairing flats, and how to drive under various slippery road conditions to avoid skids. Also, learn how to obtain the maximum mileage from each tire. For your free copy of *Consumer Tire Guide*, write: Tire Industry Safety Council, Box 1801, Washington, D.C. 20013.

Nursery Rhyme Safety Booklet

Refrigerators are so nice,
For turning water into ice,
And keeping food cold for a spell
Is what they do so very well.

If you should find one open wide,
Close it; don't ever hide inside.
Little kids who so explore
Are never heard from anymore!

This is one of the many safety jingles in the cartoon-illustrated booklet *Let's Learn About Safety.* Published by Lilly, the booklet gets through to tiny tots on a variety of safety themes—climbing trees, traffic signals, fooling around with Dad's power tools, sampling items in the medicine chest, etc. The pictures and verses orient your child about safety rules he will always remember. To obtain, send requests to: Eli Lilly and Co., Dept. TW, Indianapolis, Ind. 46206.

Lead Poisoning

Despite the fact that paints for interior use no longer contain harmful quantities of lead, children in the home can still be exposed to lead poisoning. To learn how to detect the symptoms and know the preventive measures, write for the pamphlet *Facts About Lead and Pediatrics,* to: Lead Industries Assn., 292 Madison Ave., New York, N.Y. 10017.

Solve the Drinking Problem

This 42-page booklet, *Young People and AA,* features case histories of young alcoholics. It points out danger signals for young drinkers and discusses methods of action for drinking problems. Write to: General Service Office of Alcoholics Anonymous, Box 459, Grand Central Sta., New York, N.Y. 10017.

Disaster Preparedness

In Time of Emergency: A Citizen's Handbook on Nuclear Attack, Natural Disasters contains personal and family preparedness information. Available from local or state civil defense agencies, or from: Defense Civil Preparedness Agency, The Pentagon, Washington, D.C. 20301, H-14.

First Aid for Poisoning

How can you help a conscious or unconscious victim? What can you do until he or she arrives at the hospital? Find these and other answers in a leaflet given free at any Red Cross Chapter in the country. Also available free are a variety of first aid leaflets and swimming posters plus first aid courses in Cardiopulmonary-Resuscitation, swimming, and nursing.

How to Save a Choking Victim

You are having dinner with a friend and suddenly a bone gets stuck in his throat or food gets sucked into his windpipe. Don't panic! Follow instructions on the card "How to Save a Choking Victim." Diagrams may help you save a life. For free card, write: Public Relations Dept., Aetna Life & Casualty, 151 Farmington Ave., Hartford, Conn. 06156.

Free—From Metropolitan Life

This current catalog offers a comprehensive chart about communicable diseases. To keep the record straight a free family immunization card is available and a 15 × 18-inch poster on immunization. Know early warnings of heart attack—this may save your life. 17 × 22-inch poster shows areas of first warning signals of pain and discomfort. Learn basic steps of Cardiopulmonary-Resuscitation. Illustrated in 17 × 22-inch "Life Support" poster. Write for free catalog and posters to: Health and Safety Education Division, Metropolitan Life Insurance Co., One Madison Ave., New York, N.Y. 10010.

For the Love of Bike

For Americans of all ages, from 8 to 80, the bike is back. As a result more accidents are happening, because bicycle riders are not paying enough attention to basic traffic safety rules. An illustrated booklet, *Bike It—Safely*, lists the most important rules for bicycle safety. There are laws you must obey and there are safety tips you should know to avoid accidents. A valuable section describes maintenance of various parts, from chain to warning device. So for happy two-wheeling, request this booklet from: Communications and Public Affairs Dept., D-1, Kemper Insurance Cos., Long Grove, Ill. 60049.

Rabies

Although today rabies seldom results in human fatalities, it remains a potentially dangerous public health problem. Each year more than 30,000 Americans have to undergo rabies treatments as a result of exposure to potentially rabid animals. Did you know that all warm-blooded animals can spread rabies, including skunks, foxes, bats, domestic farm animals, and domestic pets, such as dogs and cats? What should you do if bitten? What can be done to prevent rabies? Do you know how to vaccinate your pet to protect him from rabies? For all the facts, read *Rabies*. You can obtain a free copy by sending a stamped, *long*, self-addressed envelope to: American Veterinary Medical Assn., 930 N. Meacham Rd., Schaumburg, Ill. 60196.

Fire Safety Manual

Will you be one of the 8,000 Americans who will die in a home fire this year? The tragic fact is that most of these victims will not burn to death, but will die in bed from smoke, toxic gases, or lack of oxygen. Thousands of Americans die needlessly because they react counterproductively when they discover a fire. Many waste precious minutes trying to put out a fire before awakening the family or calling the fire department. Others open hot doors, attempt to dash through thick smoke, or, in panic, fail to think of the most obvious measures for escape. For a life-saving *Fire Safety Manual* which tells you how to make your home virtually fireproof and discusses home fire-detection methods and inexpensive alarms, write to: Dynamics, 2015 Ivy Rd., Box 5689, Charlottesville, Va. 22903.

Stop, Thief!

There is no way you can make make your home 100% burglarproof. But there are a number of simple, inexpensive things you can do to minimize the chances that a burglar will pick your home as his target, and protect yourself in case he does. A booklet, *The Adventures of Surelocked Homes*, tells how to make things tough for the thief, set a trap for him, what to do if you meet the burglar, what to do if you're burglarized. Free from: State Farm and Casualty Co., Bloomington, Ill. 61701.

Know Someone Who Steals?

Shoplifters go to jail! Policemen, juveniles, officers, youth groups, teachers, store executives, use the message of this book to help shoplifters stop. Help a shoplifter quit by sending for this free book, *Danger—Hands Off*, to: International Lutheran Layman's League, 2185 Hampton Ave., St. Louis, Mo. 63139.

Before the Emergency

It is estimated that 20,000 Americans die needlessly and 25,000 more are permanently injured at the scene of accidents because of inadequate emergency medical care. It is worth every dollar, every hour, every effort your community can expend to bring swift and skillful help to people in urgent need. A booklet, *Community Action . . . Before the Emergency*, describes how your community can gear up to help people fast. Write: Public Relations Div., Employers Insurance of Wausau, Wausau, Wis. 54401.

For Safe TV Viewing

Is television harmful to the eyes? Is it safe for children to sit up close to the set? Is it all right to watch TV in a dark room? What special rules should you observe when watching color television? You'll find the answers to these, and many other pertinent questions regarding TV-watching, in a scientifically accurate pamphlet, *To View . . . or Not to View*? To obtain, send a stamped, self-addressed, *long* envelope to: Communications Division, American Optometric Association, 243 North Lindbergh Blvd., St. Louis, Mo. 63141.

If You Drink and Drive

Drinking and driving are a deadly combination. In fact, alcohol abuse is listed as a factor in up to 50% of fatal automobile accidents. To help drivers understand the relationship between consumption and accident involvement, and to show you the fallacy of the old "one for the road" custom, imbibers should read *The Way to Go,* a factual summary of the latest information on the fatal habits of those who are soused while steering. It may well shake you up, and get you to shake off John Barleycorn. Free from: Communications and Public Affairs Dept., D-1, Kemper Insurance Cos., Long Grove, Ill. 60049.

Free Emergency Telephone Number Card

This free *Home Safety Checklist* is a 30-point reminder to help you keep your home accident-free. Lists common hazards and dangers in living room, bedroom, kitchen, garage, bathroom, and basement that can *easily* be avoided. Review it quickly and often. Reverse side is an easy-to-spot emergency telephone number card on which you can list numbers of fire department, police, nearest neighbor, doctor, etc. To obtain, write to: Travelers Insurance Co., Women's Information Bureau H-1, 1 Tower Sq., Hartford, Conn. 06115.

Hazards in the Home

Every year thousands of people die from the effects of toxic gases and vapors and from swallowing or absorbing through the skin poisonous materials commonly found around the home. Tragically, many of these deaths are children under 5 years old. A free booklet, *Silent Menace in and Around Your Home* will alert you on how to avoid explosions, toxic plants, toxic gases, poisons, and burns from common substances in your home. Write: Communications and Public Affairs Dept., D-1, Kemper Insurance Cos., Long Grove, Ill. 60049.

Food Safety

Come summertime you may not be able to do much about the ants that invade your picnic, but you can prevent an invasion of bacteria that may cause food poisoning. The best preventive is to take along good food-handling habits on every outing that includes food. The place to begin is when you buy the food: pick up meat and poultry products last at the supermarket, have the clerk pack them all together so they will stay cool longer, and take them straight home to the refrigerator or freezer. Use a well-insulated cooler and plenty of ice to keep foods cold on the outing and be sure to cook meats and poultry thoroughly over the barbecue coals. For more summertime food handling tips, write to: Information Div., Animal and Plant Health Inspection Service, U.S. Dept. of Agriculture, Washington, D.C. 20250. Ask for the fact bulletin *Summertime Food Safety*.

Television Safety Tips

The TV set, a permanent fixture in almost every American home, is also a potential source of danger if not installed, serviced, and maintained properly. Thousands each year unwittingly expose themselves to fire hazards, severe electrical shocks, and even electrocution, because of improper use. A booklet, *Television Safety Tips*, lists 22 danger points to watch out for when using your set. To obtain, send a *long*, self-addressed, stamped envelope to: Electronic Industries Assn., P.O. Box 19369, Washington, D.C. 20036.

23

A GOLDEN AGE FOR SENIOR CITIZENS

We've come up with gifts for babies, teenagers, college lads, brides and grooms, wage earners, business executives. Now it's time we turned the spotlight on the folks in the twilight years of their lives. To enrich their retirement age, and to assure them that this period we must all enter some day can be active and fruitful, this chapter is respectfully dedicated.

Free Florida Facts

Interested in retiring? A 16-page booklet, *Facts About Florida Retirement,* shows the advantages of Florida living for retired persons, with information about the state. It discusses Florida tax advantages, recreation facilities, making social contacts, and cultural activities, and gives a checklist for real-estate buyers. There is also a chart entitled "People Live Longer in Florida," showing the high life-expectancy figures for the state's residents. To obtain, write to: Florida Development Commission, Gaines and Adams Sts., Tallahassee, Fla. 32301.

Diets for Old Folks

Senior citizens, because of their sedentary existence, loss of teeth, and changes in the digestive tract, require different menus from their more active and younger neighbors. For an excellent guide to good eating habits write for the Department of Agriculture's *Food Guide for Older Folks*, bulletin G-17. To obtain, send 50¢ to cover mailing and handling to: Superintendent of Documents, U.S. Government Printing Office, Washington, D.C. 20402.

For Middle-aged Feet

Too many Americans walk into middle age on feet that are just about ready to break down under the job of carrying them around. If you are 50 years or older, a helpful folder, *Middle-Aged Feet*, can solve most of your walking problems. To obtain, send a stamped, self-addressed envelope to: N.Y. State Podiatry Society, Statler-Hilton Hotel, Seventh Ave. and 33rd St., New York, N.Y. 10001.

Meals on Wheels

In many localities scattered throughout the country, the U.S. Department of Health, Education, and Welfare serves *Meals on Wheels*, a daily hot dinner brought to elderly people who live alone and cannot get out to shop. You needn't feel embarrassed to avail yourself of this service—it's your right. Phone the department's regional office in your area (Information will provide you with the telephone number) and find out if they can accommodate you.

Retiring Plans

If you plan to retire soon, a new government booklet can help you decide how to spend your time, whether to live in your present community or move to another one, and whether to change to a new type of housing. Also discussed are how to set up a realistic and flexible budget, estimating expenses and financial resources, and where and how to live for your income and satisfaction. To obtain a copy of *A Guide to Budgeting for the Retired Couple*, request Publication G-194 and send 45¢ to: Superintendent of Documents, U.S. Government Printing Office, Washington, D.C. 20402.

Retirement Booklet

Thinking about retirement? Wondering how to plan so that you'll be able to make the most of our "golden years"? If your answer is yes, then this booklet is for you. For a copy of *Not by Chance,* write: ITT, Community Development Corporation, Palm Coast, Fla. 32038.

Travel Tips for Senior Citizens

International travel can be a rich and rewarding experience—or it can be a nightmare. A minimum of preparation can help make your visit a trouble-free, memorable adventure. This pamphlet includes information on passports and visas, where to convert currency, health aids, clothing tips, and other facts you should know to make your trip a merry one. For a free brochure write: Travel Tips for Senior Citizens, Bureau of Consular Affairs, U.S. Dept. of State, Publication 8970, Washington, D.C. 20402.

For the Denture Crowd

Do your dentures slip? Do they irritate you? Gould All-Day, Inc., offers a free packet, containing 6 all-day denture adhesive cushions, as a temporary aid to hold dentures in place. For free packet, write: Gould All-Day, Inc., Mamaroneck, N.Y. 10543.

Optometric Fees

How does the optometrist determine his fee? Why do your glasses cost more than your sister's? Should you ask the optometrist to quote a fee before the examination? What does a service fee include? Are optometric fees covered by government health plans? Are visual aids tax deductible? Answers to questions that you've always wanted to ask your optometrist but never dared can be found in this pamphlet entitled *A R E You Seeing Straight About Optometric Fees?* For a free copy, send a 10-inch long, stamped, self-addressed envelope to: Communications Division, American Optometric Association, 243 North Lindbergh Blvd., St. Louis, Mo. 63141.

About Cataracts

A common condition if you're past 40. This booklet has information on cataracts plus a glossary to acquaint you with medical terms. To obtain free copy, send self-addressed, stamped #10 envelope to: "Your Cataract," IOLAB Corp., 695 West Terrace Dr., San Dimas, Calif. 91773.

Can't Drink Milk?

If you are one of the 30 million Americans who can't drink milk because of the inability to digest the natural milk sugar, lactose, you can receive a 4-quart trial-size sample of new liquid LactAid. LactAid is an enzyme derived from natural sources which, when added to milk, converts the lactose into simple sugars for easy digestibility. For free 4-quart trial sample, send $1.00 for postage and handling to: LactAid, SugarLo Co., 3540 Atlantic Ave., P.O. Box 1017, Atlantic City, N.J. 08404.

82 Tax Facts for Older Americans

This comprehensive tax guide will give persons nearing or of retirement age a summary of the major state and federal tax provisions which will assist them in choosing their place of retirement. It also gives information on the tax concessions, such as state and federal retirement income credits, that the state and federal governments grant to the elderly. This guide also tells how far the various states have gone to ease, through tax concessions, some of the financial problems of those retiring on low, fixed incomes. Prepared by the National Retired Teachers Association and American Association of Retired Persons, the booklet also includes information on property and sales taxes as well as special exemptions and deductions for older people. Write: NRTA-AARP, P.O. Box 2400, Long Beach, Calif. 90802.

Save Your Sight

If you're half a century old or older, we have bad news and good news for you. The bad news is that as we age we are prone to develop such conditions of the eyes as presbyopia, glaucoma, and cataract. The good news is that, if detected in time, most of these problems can be treated and controlled. Remember, your eyes are rationed, two to a lifetime, so send for the free booklet *Your Vision, the Second 50 Years*. To obtain, send a *long*, self-addressed, stamped envelope to: Communications Division, American Optometric Association, 243 North Lindbergh Blvd., St. Louis, Mo. 63141.

Retirement Guides

A series of informative "better retirement" guides for older Americans is being offered by the National Retired Teachers Association and American Association of Retired Persons. The series includes:

> *Retirement Housing Guide*
> *Retirement Legal Guide*
> *Retirement Health Guide*
> *Retirement Food Guide*
> *Retirement Safety Guide*
> *Retirement Moving Guide*
> *Retirement Anti-Crime Guide*
> *Retirement Pet Guide*

To obtain any of the above, write to: NRTA-AARP, P.O. Box 2400, Long Beach, Calif. 90802.

Preretirement Guides

A series of informative guidebooks designed for persons in the 50 to 65 age group is being offered free by Action for Independent Maturity (AIM), the preretirement planning division of the American Association of Retired Persons. The series includes:

AIM's Health Guide to Independent Living
AIM's Legal Guide to Independent Living
AIM's Leisure Guide to Independent Living

To obtain any of these guidebooks, write to: AIM, 1909 K St., NW, Washington, D.C. 20049.

BritRail Travel Pass for Senior Citizens

BritRail Travel International Inc. offers a Senior Citizen BritRail Pass, which will afford to those age 65 or older first class travel at the economy class rate. As with the Youth Pass, the sole criterion will be that of age to be verified from the customer's passport. For more information, write: BritRail Travel International, 630 Third Ave., New York, N.Y. 10017.

Golden Age Passport

What is it? What is it good for? Where do you get it? If you are 62 years of age or older this "Golden Age" passport is your free lifetime entrance ticket to all federal recreation programs. For brochure full of information, write for *Golden Age Passports* to: Consumer Information Center, No. 631 G, Pueblo, Colo. 81009.

Guidebook for Widowed Persons

On Being Alone, a guidebook for the widowed and those who counsel widowed persons, provides practical advice on living through bereavement, personal and social adjustment, financial and legal affairs, and housing and household management. Written by Dr. James A. Peterson, professor of sociology at the University of Southern California and a marriage and family counselor, this informative guidebook is published by Action for Independent Maturity (AIM), a division of the 9 million-member American Association of Retired Persons. Write: AIM, Dept. M, 1909 K St., NW, Washington, D.C. 20049.

Personal Crime Prevention

Although crime is reportedly on the increase, you needn't be one of its unfortunate victims. In *Your Retire-*

ment Anticrime Guide you'll find tips on tactics you can use to avoid being taken by con artists or mugged in the street. It also contains advice on how to be safe when you open the door and on making your home safe from burglars. For a copy, write: NRTA-AARP, P.O. Box 2400, Long Beach, Calif. 90802.

24

FREE FILMS FOR YOUR PROJECTOR

If you are one of the millions of Americans who own a 16-mm movie projector—there are miles of free reels for you! It's an amazing screenland stockpile you are cordially invited to share. And all this entertainment is free. Who produces these films? Business firms make them to foster good public relations for their products or services. Tourist agencies sponsor them to stimulate traveling. So do various agencies which want to reach people with that great education tool—celluloid. You can arrange to show these stimulating films in your school, lodge, church, businessmen's group, union, civic group, youth center, or political club. And now . . . on to "Little Hollywood."

16-mm Features

The following films are available on loan to all adult community groups, women's clubs, churches, and high-school and university instructors. The user pays *return postage* only. To obtain, specify the *title* and the *number* of the film you want, and send requests to: Association-Sterling Films, 600 Grand Ave., Ridgefield, N.J. 07657. All films are 16-mm and have sound tracks.

Art Is (S-503). Conductor Leonard Bernstein, ballet master Edward Villella, artist Robert Murray, and mime Tony Montanaro are featured in this award-winning color

film, which contains some new answers to the age-old
question—"What is art?" 28 mins. (Presented by the Asso-
ciated Councils of the Arts and the Sears-Roebuck Foundation.)

For the Love of An Eagle (2669). This filmed record, in
color, of a young South African woman's encounter with
the rare black eagle, is far more than a documentary on
animal conservation. It is, in fact, a love story. With sym-
pathy and concern, Jean Cowden fights these proud animals' distrust of humans, provides food and protection for
a newborn, and finally wins the family's friendship. Told
in her own words, as she lived it on a remote mountaintop
in South Africa, this film is a compelling perspective of
what can be done to preserve our natural resources by
people who care. (Presented by Information Service of
South Africa.)

Chinese Costumes (G-284). An oriental fashion show
exhibiting costumes from the past on down to modern
design. Included are scenes of various periods showing
clothes and costumes worn by the figures of the day, such
as the military, Tartars, emperors, and their courtiers,
There are fascinating glimpses of ornamental hairpins,
fingernail coverings, jewelry, dragon robes, and crowns in
brilliant color. 21 mins. (Presented by the Chinese Information Service.)

France on Wheels (2415). Follow three pretty girls
through France on the super all-electric train *Le Capitole*.
Besides the scenery of Nice, Corsica, Strasbourg Cathedral, Fontainebleau, Chartres Cathedral, and the races at
Deauville, we see facilities such as movies, discotheques,
beauty parlors, and fashion shows—right on the train. 27
mins.

Japan Season-by-Season (F-222). This breathtaking beautiful film depicts the enchanting natural beauty of Japan
throughout the seasons of the year. Revolving around this
central theme, the film covers very many aspects of Japanese life and culture in country and city, including traditional arts, festivals, and modern history—in short, the
essence of Japan.

We Came In Peace (S-918). Man's dream of conquering
space is developed in this definitive color documentary of
space exploration from Jules Verne to the moon landing

by the Apollo 11 astronauts. Historical footage shows the triumphs and tragedies of the U.S. space program as well as early experiments in rocketry by Robert Goddard, the wartime use of German V-2 rockets, and the first successful spaceflight, by a Russian cosmonaut. "Gold" Award, International Film and Television Festival of New York. 38 mins. (Presented by Gulf Oil Corporation.)

Sports Films

Great Moments in the History of Tennis (2640). Watch some of tennis's greatest moments in this intriguing film containing old movie clips that recapture the highlights of the sport. It traces the game from its origin in England in 1874, and follows its development to the present time. Featured are all-time male tennis stars and many of the women greats like Billie Jean King and Althea Gibson. 40 mins. (Presented by Philip Morris.)

Instant Replay (2481). Jerry Kramer, All-Pro tackle of the Green Bay Packers, tells the story of the Packers' sensational, unforgettable 1967 season. Coach Vince Lombardi emerged as professional football's greatest mentor as his team beat the Dallas Cowboys for the NFL championship and the Oakland Raiders, the American Football League champions, in the second Super Bowl. In color. 21 mins.

Happiness is Skiing! (S-645). On the snowy slopes of beautiful Colorado, a typical young family and Olympic champion Othmar Schneider show the many exciting facets of skiing. A color film to interest skiers and nonskiers alike. 28 mins. (Presented by Sears, Roebuck, & Co.)

21 Days in May (J-976). The month of May at the Indianapolis Speedway is a month of decisions—of cars, drivers, equipment, racing techniques. This action-packed color film captures the excitement and tension as irreversible decisions are made. It includes race-day festivities and driving competition as the chosen 33 drive their magnificent machines in one of the greatest racing spectacles in the world. 25 mins. (Courtesy of Firestone.)

Outdoor Films

To order any of these exciting outdoor films, specify the title of the film you wish to borrow and send your request to: Zebco Films, Modern Talking Picture Service, 1145 N. McCadden Pl., Los Angeles, Calif. 90038.

Uncle Homer, Big John and Mister Bass. Homer Circle, angling editor of *Sports Afield,* and professional bass fisherman John Powell illustrate favorite casting and bass fishing techniques using Zebco tackle under all conditions in all types of water. Instructional as well as entertaining. 25 mins.

Manitoba Fish Tale. Billy Westmoreland and Butch Harris travel to the remote lakes of Manitoba to catch fighting smallmouth bass. Along the way they encounter breathtaking scenic beauty in the romantic Canadian wilderness with an untarnished peek at wildlife in their own backyard. Plenty of smallmouth fishing with side excursions for northern pike, Winnipeg perch, and wildeye provide angling action to keep expert and novice alike entertained. 30 mins.

All-American Bass. Features professional bass fishing champion Roland Martin and Chuck Roberts taking on the wily largemouth of Lake Stockton, Missouri. Includes in-depth instruction on today's bass fishing techniques. Great underwater sequences. 35 mins.

Archery—an Introduction. Up-to-date shooting techniques, both bare bow and sight, outlining the basic steps to top shooting form. 18 mins.

Devils of the Desert. Ben Pearson and his companions hunt Arizona's javelina. The film features one of the most spectacular bow-hunting shots ever recorded. 13½ mins.

Zinave. A bow-hunting safari in Mozambique where Jim Dougherty hunts a wide variety of game and takes on the dangerous Cape buffalo. 25 mins.

FAA Audiovisual Materials

The Federal Aviation Administration has available a free 20-page *FAA Film Catalog* which lists current FAA motion picture films and audio-slide packets available to the public. To obtain, send requests to: U.S. Department of Transportation, Publications and Forms Section, TAD-443.1, Washington, D.C. 20590.

How to Save Your Life in Fire and Smoke

Two Steps to Survival is available in two versions, a 19½-minute film for classroom use and a 27-minute film for T.V. *Get Low and Get Out* is a 7-minute film describing latest school smoke drill developed by National Smoke, Fire and Burn Institute. Package consists of film, teachers guide, and posters. Films available in 16-mm or three-quarter-inch video-cassette for free loan to public. For loan information, write or call: Aetna Life & Casualty, Hartford, Conn. 06156. Tel. (203) 273-2843.

Casual China

Lenox, famous for fine china and crystal, has an exciting program designed especially for women's clubs. This program features their film *You Always Have the Nicest Parties*, illustrating Temper-ware, the most popular freezer-to-oven-to-table-to-dishwasher casual china on the market today. You will also receive, free of charge, a complete kit including press releases, ideas for presenting this program to your club, and, for handing out to your members, recipe books prepared in cooperation with *Gourmet* magazine. To receive this free 16-mm, 18-minute sound/color film and kit, write: Ellen Lynch, Director, Women's Club Activities, Lenox, Prince and Meade Sts., Trenton, N.J. 08605. All you pay is return postage on the film. Please allow 6 weeks' advance notice.

ABOUT THE AUTHORS

THELMA WEISINGER is the wife of the late MORT WEISINGER, author of the first eleven editions of *1001 Valuable Things You Can Get Free*. She has helped research and write the previous editions. Mrs. Weisinger resides in Great Neck, New York.

We Deliver!
And So Do These Bestsellers.

MS READ-a-thon–
a simple way
to start youngsters reading.

Boys and girls between 6 and 14 can join the MS READ-a-thon and help find a cure for Multiple Sclerosis by reading books. And they get two rewards — the enjoyment of reading, and the great feeling that comes from helping others.

Parents and educators: For complete information call your local MS chapter, or call toll-free (800) 243-6000. Or mail the coupon below.

Kids can help, too!

SAVE $2.00 ON YOUR NEXT BOOK ORDER!

BANTAM BOOKS 🐓

Shop-at-Home ——
Catalog

Now you can have a complete, up-to-date catalog of Bantam's inventory of over 1,600 titles—including hard-to-find books.

And, you can <u>save $2.00</u> on your next order by taking advantage of the money–saving coupon you'll find in this illustrated catalog. Choose from fiction and non-fiction titles, including mysteries, historical novels, westerns, cookbooks, romances, biographies, family living, health, and more. You'll find a description of most titles. Arranged by categories, the catalog makes it easy to find your favorite books and authors and to discover new ones.

So don't delay—send for this shop-at-home catalog and save money on your next book order.

Just send us your name and address and 50¢ to defray postage and handling costs.

CHOOSE YOUR OWN ADVENTURE ®

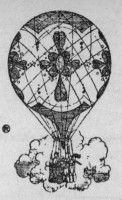

You'll want all the books in the exciting *Choose Your Own Adventure*® series offering you hundreds of fantasy adventures without ever leaving your chair. Each book takes you through an adventure—under the sea, in a space colony, on a volcanic island—in which you become the main character. What happens next in the story depends on the choices *you* make and *only you* can decide how the story ends!